POWERHOUSE

ISBN 978-0-9898465-1-6

Find more resources and training for
Pastors, Worship Pastors,
and Creative Arts Ministries at
Downpourintl.com

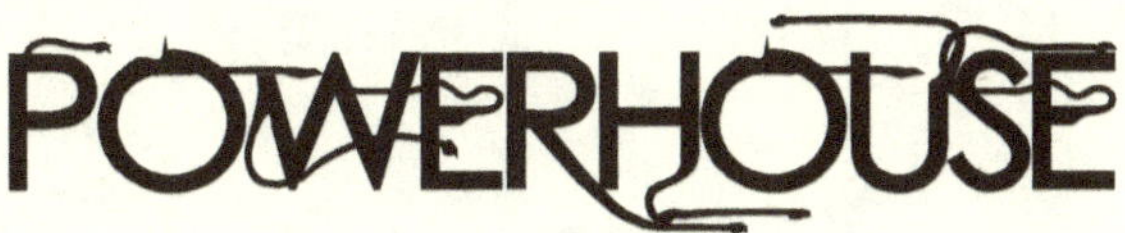

The Essential Steps to Produce a Powerful Performance

~ Become a Strong Leader ~

~ Build Powerful Rehearsals ~

~ Experience God's Presence ~

Ken Jansen

Downpour International Publishing

CONTENTS

ACKNOWLEDGEMENTS

My deepest thanks and adoration go to my beautiful wife Anna. Without you by my side, the world would be a dreary place. Thank you for your encouragement, optimism and support. I could not have accomplished this without you. May I be a courageous husband and father for our family.

Thank you to my loving family, especially my parents - Ron and Debbie. Your guidance, and many sacrifices, put me on a path towards a great calling that only Jesus could have imagined. Your support in my life has been more than I ever deserved.

Thank you to my incredible Grandfather, Kenneth Crocker. The way you lived out Jesus' call on your life has forever influenced mine. You taught me everything about ministry by your heart for others and passion to serve the Lord.

Thank you to the many teachers who have mentored me through the years. John Hayward, Sharon Wilkins, Calvin Johansson, Richard Honea, Sam Gordon. I could never have imagined the wealth of knowledge you shared with me. I hope to do the same for others.

Thank you to the hundreds of church worship department team members who have served with me through the years. Your desire to be used by God has allowed me to develop into the leader He called me to be.

Thank you to my Lord and Savior, Jesus Christ, for saving this reckless heart of mine. My path has been unknown but exciting, exhausting but fulfilling, strenuous yet designed. I promise to continue this journey wherever You may lead. Guide my steps that I may reach the lost for You, until the whole world understands the joy in Worshiping You.

INTRODUCTION

It was just a few days into August, 2006 when a young man, fresh out of school, moved several states away to accept his first full-time position as Worship Pastor of a fairly large and established church. The pastor of this church had pursued the young man to take on this role for over 3 years. Anytime the young man sought an answer as to if this was the right step, there was always a hesitation and something that held back the ability to accept. But now it was clear that God had positioned everything in just the right way for the answer to be, "YES!" It was time to take the job. The young man packed up all his belongings, instruments, books, hopes and dreams and was ready to make a difference in the world. It all started in a large church building sitting in the middle of a small town.

The move was long and arduous, halfway across the US, from the North all way to the southern coast. It took 2 days to get there driving a 20ft long U-Haul truck towing a car transport behind with an old Jeep ready for new territory. The road was hot, the air was humid, but for the young man it couldn't stifle the anticipation and excitement of his first full-time position. He was going to be making a "salary" and thoughts were swirling around his mind. He thought of all he could do with the finances, how he would make a name for himself in the world and be welcomed in this new area as a servant of God's kingdom. The years of school and preparation had finally led to this step. It was like a crescendo of hard work and anticipation. This was the goal of all he worked hard to achieve. His older brother helped him pack the truck, he sweat through the summer miles alongside him until they finally unpacked the truck and it was time to go. The young man took his brother to the airport, said goodbye and drove back to his new home to get to work. He was truly excited and filled with a wonder like Christmas morning. What would come next in this new adventure?

Thursday night came quickly. It was time for the band to practice. The man fully planned out the rehearsal and went over the songs a hundred times to make sure it would be setting a precedent for worship rehearsals and services to come. This was a new era of leadership in the church, a time that would be signified by his very own arrival and tenure. With such an opportunity, and he didn't want to leave any margin for error. The rehearsal went well and was filled with energy, laughing and smiles. Everyone seemed happy with new relationships and possibilities of what God was going to do. As the team parted and said goodbye from the parking lot, a calm feeling of accomplishment came over the young man. He had done his best and felt secure in his decision to take the job, move across the country, and dive into this new adventure. He was ready and able to do what God called him to do.

And then…

After returning home, it wasn't 10 minutes before the young man got a call from the lead pastor. A musician from the worship team rehearsal, who happened to be his daughter, called to inform him that, "the rehearsal wasn't good enough for their caliber of performance on a Sunday morning." Hearing those words were like a blast of cold electricity coursing through the young man. He was utterly shocked and taken back. He thought, "I've never encountered something like this. What should I do? What should I say?" A gigantic weight developed in his stomach that turned and remained stationary at the same time. He was nauseous, embarrassed, felt a tingling throughout his body and felt as though a spotlight was shining on him that he couldn't escape. He was instructed to give the young girl a call, painfully investigate what her thoughts and reasoning could be for reporting such news to the lead pastor, develop a new strategy for a winning rehearsal and service on Sunday morning, AND somehow admit to some sort of wrong-doing to the entire team, many of whom were just beginning to build their impressions of the new young man as a leader.

You may be asking who the young man was? Well, this is part of my story, and this chapter remains one of my worst memories in ministry. And I mean it haunted me in recurring nightmares for a long time. I felt like a failure and everyone's eyes were on me, watching me underperform and let everyone down. I didn't know whom I could to turn to. My family was more than 1,000 miles away and obviously couldn't meet with me in person. I did my best to build relationships, but I didn't have any close friends in the church as I was brand new to the area. The only friends I did have were the very same people on the teams I worked with. Any respect, trust or welcoming I had hoped for from the team and new church family had been taken away and replaced by harsh criticism, gossip and nepotism. I'd done everything I knew to do.

I enacted everything I was taught from numerous music professors, my own pastoral experience and training from ministry leaders. I did my best to create a welcoming environment for every person serving there. I set goals, rehearsed parts, wrote new charts, questioned current and past team members so I could bring out familiar favorites of the congregation... But unfortunately, there were many other negative factors in the environment I would soon learn about.

I was caught unaware. In my time to visit and interview for the position, 2 times within 3 years in fact, I never saw the depth and gravity of the tension in the relationships. I didn't know how to deal with the weight of my responsibilities, let alone the verbal abuse I received and the lack of support from leadership and volunteers alike. I soon fell into a depression and habit of stress management that lasted me for years. I led rehearsals for services on Sunday morning, Sunday night, Wednesday night and other extra events. I had on average 4-5 rehearsals a week with 3-5 services, not including playing and singing for funerals. Every week of serving at that church, I could almost feel the joy being sucked out my passion and calling. It was by far the worst year of my life.

I wish the me of today could speak to the me of August, 2006. I would tell that young man, "It's ok. You've done well. God has gifted you beyond what you can imagine and prepared you for this very day. You ARE NOT ALONE! I AM HERE WITH YOU AND WILL NOT LEAVE YOU! Though it may feel like you are isolated, ashamed, unable, and stuck between a rock and hard place, I will walk with you in every step to help you see the Freedom God has given you. I will teach you how to "See the Field" in ministry to know exactly what you're dealing with. I will teach you the skills to challenge everyone around you, even musicians who are more advanced and experienced than you are right now. I will be your lifeline and your advocate in building trust in your church, trust with your team, and especially trust with your pastor. We walk through this together. You will grow, learn, and build on what you already know and what you can do. Do NOT worry. Every great leader goes through challenging seasons. This may be one of your greatest challenges, but you are going to sail through this with flying colors. You will be so strong, capable, comfortable, influential and confident when we take the next step. Listen to me and we're going to get through this together. Let's make this one of the most exciting and life-building times of your life!"

Who wouldn't love to hear words of encouragement like that when you step into Life's unknown? This is what I want to give to you. Reading this book is the first part of this skill-building path and soul-forging encouragement. I pray right now that you would read that last paragraph and imagine I am speaking those words to you. I believe God has given me experiences and a great opportunity to share hope, encouragement, and training to musicians and servants around the world. I want to be your lifeline and hope to give you the support and care I wish I would've had in the beginning years of my ministry.

What's the point of a Powerful Rehearsal?

If you're leading any sort of service at a church, you obviously want God's presence to be there in a mighty way. How many services have you lead, or visited as a non-leader where you walked away wishing there was more? It's okay to answer that question for yourself in the desire that we want to find a reason for wanting more and determine a pathway to produce a greater experience. What an incredible opportunity we have as ministry leaders and servants to be able to work alongside our

Heavenly Father to draw others into God's presence. The fact is that a Powerful Worship Service is created by many different factors, most all of those happen before the actual service ever starts.

Contributing Factors for a Powerful Worship Service include;

1. Spiritual Unity in the church and use of Familiar and Favorite Worship songs or anthems
2. New and Exciting aspects for people to look forward to, i.e. - New Songs, God Speaking a New Word and giving Focus to the church leadership
3. Recognition of how God is moving in this church
4. Joyful Fellowship and Connections within the church body
5. Ministry Focused Campaigns for building God's Kingdom and the church as a whole
6. The Support of all church attendees in the service
7. A Powerful Rehearsal that prepares all those involved in producing the Worship Service

My desire is to layout all of the steps for you in this book. I want every service and performance your team is involved in to be blessed in a mighty way. I want you to be able to walk away from each time you sing or play and say, "Wow, I know that God is here and this is where I want to be all the time." In order for you to learn what is necessary to create an ongoing encounter like that, I must first teach you how to Build a Powerful Rehearsal.

Rehearsal Overview

There's just no getting around it. Whether you're starting your path as a worship leader, you've been leading worship for more than 20 years, or you're stepping in to cover for a leader as they take vacation, at some point you will need to have a rehearsal. In all my years of leading teams for different ministry groups and churches of varying size, I've found that Powerful Rehearsals are vital to the success and preparedness of your team. Of course, I've had those few occasions where no one was able to come to practice even after multiple schedule changes, and the stars aligned to bring the perfect storm of sickness / special events in town / and family birthdays that prevented anyone from making a rehearsal time. Even in the times where a practice during the week wasn't possible, I've still always made sure to have a light rehearsal before service or the performance time to make sure everyone is on the same page. Small teams to large teams, beginning musicians to studio recording artists, we all need time to get a "feel" for what is expected and what can happen when we gather together.

I believe every worship leader has "Vision." God has called us to lead people into His presence, and

Proverbs 29:18 "Where there is no vision, the people perish"

Speaking of all worship leaders as a collective, we have a beautiful and unfinished picture in our minds of our church. We can see what the lights look like on the stage, the arrangement of the band, what songs will be played and an idea of the intimate response from the congregation. This response is created by many qualities of each individual song and element in the service.

There are no words to describe when an amazing atmosphere is crafted, resulting in almost a crescendo of lives being submitted to a new revelation of who God is. If you experience a vision similar to this on a weekly basis as you plan your services, you are not alone. God is surely giving something amazing to your church family and there are ways to promote this kind of atmosphere as a common culture. On the other hand, if you're reading this description of service planning and you could only hope to have a fraction of this kind of passion and energy welling up within you as you try to bring together some sort of creative aspect to Sunday… then I want you to know you are not alone! There are many churches around the world blessed with talent and skill however they are devoid of passion and energy.

Service planning takes intentional effort and unfortunately some leaders either just don't know what to do or they put too much effort into things that inhibit them from greater rehearsals and development. I've had the opportunity to lead a large multi-site network of churches serving thousands on the weekend, and I've also served at smaller churches where the band on stage outnumbered those in the seats. You have to plan your service with a vision in mind, and then through using the organized steps outlined in this book, put into practice a sustainable method for achieving a Powerful Rehearsal which will lead to Powerful Worship Services.

A little about me…

Just to give you some background information about me, I grew up in a loving home with my grandparents being ministers. They built and pastored the first church I ever went to. I got to see both of them leading the music and preaching sermons every week. They were both incredibly talented with an undeniable call on their lives. My grandfather was an incredible artist and used to give art lessons to my brother, my sister and me. We'd sit on his knee out in his finished garage. With a large halogen lamp hung overhead, he lovingly instructed us in the art of painting and drawing. I can still see the drafting table and smell the Acrylic paints like it was yesterday. I still have a painting he helped me with, a pretty good rendition of Mowgli and Baloo from the Jungle Book. Because of the exposure to art, music and ministry at a young age, I've always been drawn to serving God in creative ways.

I was called into Worship Ministry when I was 18. I was at a Sunday night church service, which was ordinarily pretty boring… I mainly just went to see my friends and hang out at Taco Bell afterwards. But this night was different. Somewhere in the monotony of the message and songs that seemed to repeat forever, God gave me a vision. It was as clear as day. I felt like I was watching a movie on an IMAX screen but I was also on the screen while seeing every angle and aspect of the picture. I saw myself on a stage. It was dark, with some light coming from above. There were people bowing down in worship all around and God was using me to connect others to Him. I can still see it in my mind as vividly as that I saw it that night.

I was electrified. As soon as the service ended I didn't know if I should stay, run out the door, bounce off the walls, tell everyone or tell no one and try to figure out what just happened to me. I left my friends to go meet my family at a restaurant across town. I was so excited that I got a speeding ticket on the way. I wasn't sure how to interpret the vision right away, but from then on, I dreamed of becoming the next Michael W. Smith.

So, I followed God's call and attended a Christian university where I received a BM degree in Vocal Performance. I studied classical music, composition, and every class on music theory possible. I became one of the main worship leaders for the school and developed as I led worship productions on a large scale and with thousands in attendance. I then sought out God's next steps for my life, which led me to earning a Master's degree in Choral Conducting Performance, which I jokingly explain as a degree in "Crowd Management." This formal training in music has given me a deep appreciation for different kinds of music, methods of teaching, and rehearsal practices in both secular and ministry arenas.

I have been in church and around musical productions for most all of my life. With so many years of experience, I've seen and been through some of the worst rehearsal experiences imaginable. I've also had the opportunity to build up systems that produce incredible results where there were none previously.

I want to walk you through my system of building a Powerful Rehearsal, the method I've built over my 20 plus years in worship ministry. You see, I've been there. I've been the inexperienced worship leader struggling to make things happen. I've tried and struggled... and I've learned from my experiences to create a recipe for success. I've built programs including 100's of volunteers and worked through challenges of building, communicating, and executing a vision that will create environments for people to experience the love of Jesus.

Yes, you can create a rehearsal culture that is exciting! Your team will be excited through the week for the next time you get together, and they'll be driven to produce your vision.

Throughout this book I'll be sharing many of my experiences with you, ideas about who we are as "Creative People," and some of my beliefs about who God is and what He wants us to do as we serve Him and His kingdom. Following in the footsteps and Jesus and working alongside what God is doing is the ONLY way we will truly be effective leaders in our church.

My prayer as you read this book is for you to be encouraged and built up as a leader. I like to write in a conversational style, so as you read, I want you to imagine I'm just sitting down and having a chat with you as a mentor. I have always been passionate about serving, helping, and building up other leaders and now we are on a journey together. I wish someone had given me the gift of their experience when I was starting out in worship ministry. I wouldn't say I've ever failed. I don't like that word. But, I have had some incredibly hard and stressful situations I thought were just normal. Without someone to tell me, "There's an easier way to do this," I worked harder than necessary trying to fix the world when I could've spent more energy enjoying God's blessings.

I believe God wants us all to grow our skills in this life. I've been fortunate enough to experience huge success in worship ministry. I promise that these techniques and steps will work for any kind of music or church service you are leading. Through trial and error, pain and joy, I have personally developed and used this system with success over many years, and I continue to teach others this model in working with multiple churches today. I want to pass on to you ALL I've learned in worship ministry,

*There are times when you may be the only one to lead church on a weekend. Maybe the skies have blanketed the town with multiple feet of snow or floodwaters on a Sunday morning. Maybe your church's talent pool is only open on the shallow end with room for Me, Myself and I. The following steps are written for working with teams of more than 1, but these steps also serve as a healthy guide

to preparing yourself individually for leading others into worship.

The Mark of a Powerful Rehearsal

- Introduction

1. What's the point of a Powerful Rehearsal?
2. Contributing Factors for a Powerful Worship Service include;
    a. Spiritual Unity in the church and use of Familiar and Favorite Worship songs or anthems
    b. New and Exciting aspects for people to look forward to, i.e. - New Songs, God Speaking a New Word and giving Focus to the church leadership
    c. Recognition of how God is moving in this church
    d. Joyful Fellowship and Connections within the church body
    e. Ministry Focused Campaigns for building God's Kingdom and the church as a whole
    f. The Support of all church attendees in the service
    g. A Powerful Rehearsal that prepares all those involved in producing the Worship Service
3. Rehearsal Overview

13 POWERHOUSE

CHAPTER 1:

A SYSTEM FOR PLANNING

Find a Creative and Effective way to Plan

From the beginning stages of envisioning your service, to turning out the lights and locking the doors, you are the centralized gravity that draws all pieces together. We are all different in how we go about creating and that's a good thing. I personally love using software to help me plan where I want to go in a service, but sometimes I mix it up and try other tangible methods. I'm a visual learner so it's very helpful for me to see things laid out in an orderly fashion. For you this may mean getting a bunch of sticky notes, writing song names and creative elements on them, and then playing "Worship Feng-Shui" on the floor or a dry erase board, imagining the flow in your service from one element to another.

Back when I started my career as a Worship Pastor in the early 2000's, there was no such thing as Planning Center Online or many of the worship related resources readily accessible today. I had to create my own systems and build practices that would allow for organization, ease of use, and bring solutions to my challenges in planning. Let's just say that Microsoft Excel became a great friend of mine. We spent a lot of time together in those beginning years. It's a great spreadsheet program, which you can now find for free through Google Apps and a host of other software providers and even access them across all your mobile devices.

I knew that I wanted to see aggregate changes and patterns in what I was doing from week to week, month to month, and throughout my years of church ministry. Thankfully I had the foresight to know I would be planning out services for years to come and the planning I did this week would be valuable to me one, two, even five years down the road. I wanted to take my church on a journey in worship, to help them grow and let them experience songs of different genres and styles that would reach and speak to everyone attending my church. So, I created spreadsheets upon spreadsheets. I tracked song titles, artists, song themes, tempo and variations, different versions, years when the song or album was published, and of course the frequency in which we did the songs. I highly recommend keeping track of what you've done and are doing in worship because this will come in very handy later on.

Below is a picture of a typical list for one of my teams. I had developed 4 teams, each with a different name and rotating playing either for our Saturday night service times, or Sunday morning. This was a Saturday team named *Psallo*. I listed out the day and date of course, along

Sat	6.13.09	Psallo
1	B	Let God Arise
2	A	Everyone Praises
3	E	Who You Are
R1	D	Enough
R2		
O	E	Today is the Day

with our common service needs - an up-front worship set consisting of usually 3 songs, a response song after the message, and then an offertory / closing song at the end. Here you can see I kept track of the keys and song titles as a brief reminder of what this team would be doing on that weekend.

This small list picture would serve as my personal record, and then would also be emailed out to my teams for them to know the plan. I would also email the song charts in an attachment and links online to any mp3's that were available, or they could listen to CD's made available following licensing and copyright provisions.

Here is a picture of a two-week spread for my four teams with their individual songs / keys / dates etc.

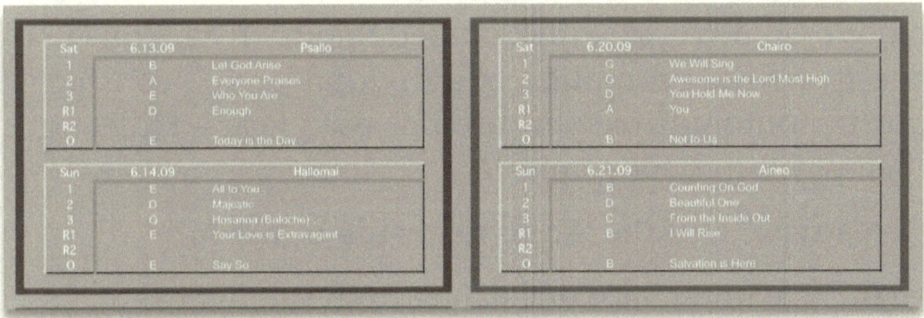

Sat	6.13.09	Psallo
1	B	Let God Arise
2	A	Everyone Praises
3	E	Who You Are
R1	D	Enough
R2		
O	E	Today is the Day

Sun	6.14.09	Hallomai
1	E	All to You
2	D	Majestic
3	G	Hosanna (Baloche)
R1	E	Your Love is Extravagant
R2		
O	E	Say So

Sat	6.20.09	Chairo
1	G	We Will Sing
2	G	Awesome is the Lord Most High
3	D	You Hold Me Now
R1	A	You
R2		
O	B	Not to Us

Sun	6.21.09	Aineo
1	B	Counting On God
2	D	Beautiful One
3	C	From the Inside Out
R1	B	I Will Rise
R2		
O	B	Salvation is Here

Just in case you are wondering, I didn't want to name my teams A team, B team etc. to show any sort of hierarchy, so I chose words in the Greek that had something to do with worship and praise.

1. *Psallo* which translated from the Greek means, "making melody."
2. *Hallomai* means, "to leap, spring up."
3. *Chairo* means, "to rejoice exceedingly."
4. *Aineo* means, "to praise, extol, and to sing praises in honor to God.

These individual team organization plans were then part of a larger list that included more information about each song. The other lists were created as tabs in the same spreadsheet for easy switching. Each song had its own information listed including; Title, Artist, Album, Year published, Tempo, Key, and Male or Female Lead. This may seem like overkill but if you are ever wondering how much new music vs. old music you are doing in church, this is a great way to see what you're incorporating into worship services on an objective basis. I've had times where I focus on building up song familiarity in our services. With planning out my sets like this, I am then able to look at the songs I'm doing and determine if I have done anything new, songs written in the last 1 - 3 years. It's a little easier now to stay current on new music in the church worship world with updated Spotify lists, YouTube channels, and the promotion of individual churches which are putting out multiple new albums each year - Hillsong and Bethel Church for example.

"Creatives" and the Analytical side of the job

Most "Creatives" are not strong in the analytical or administrative side of the job. Our personality type is typically relegated to the free-form, easy going nature of "letting things just happen" and procrastinating to the last minute. I'm not sure if I am really strong in administration and logistics naturally, or I've just learned how useful and important it is in this profession.

Communicating your vision is key to executing it with success and without good records in a worship department; your work is going to be even harder. I'm all about making things easy. I tell my clients all the time, "I create systems and processes, and provide steps to Build Powerful services. This way you don't have to reinvent the wheel every week." Having a system of past records with plans for the future is a necessary and healthy step towards effective planning.

Online Service Planning

Using an online service is great. Planning Center Online / PCO has really come a long way since its inception and has some great tools integrated today into its interface that can help your church remain copyright compliant, and also help you communicate effectively to all your teams in no time at all.

One of my favorite tools of PCO is working in the Matrix view for planning services and scheduling teams. Remember that I'm visual learner, so I definitely appreciate the Matrix view as it allows me to see as many services in the past as I want to bring up, and the same for the future. You can even drag and drop a song from a previous service to a new one and the use the same method for planning out your band members and the

frequency they play and sing.

I love using this online software platform because every time you import and setup a new song, you have all that charts, recordings, and information saved and ready to be recalled the next time you use that song. You can update the song attachments and info anytime you like. For example, you could make notes on a particular song about which key you performed last time, who was the soloist or who sang lead, if the tempo needed to be changed, how well the song was received and if changes need to be made before you perform the song again.

This tool has the ability to save you time and energy when it comes to communicating and keeping your plans organized. It keeps everyone on the same page. When I am working with large teams, any software that can make my life easier and more effective is definitely worth the investment.

If you don't have a consistent method for "planning a service," I suggest you just get over the initial discomfort of planning in advance and let God work through you. You are partnering with Him in where He wants to take your church and worship experiences. Do your part and work on finding the best methods for developing a plan.

Our God is Present in the Moment.

I am a firm believer that God can disrupt your plans and do whatever He wants in any given service at any given time. We serve a God who is alive and active right this very moment. There may be an area of an intimate worship song where God just wants you to stop, pray, repeat a chorus, or just play instrumentally to allow people to rest in His presence. As Worship Leaders, we need to be sensitive to these times, allow the Holy Spirit to speak to us, and be obedient to what God wants to do. After all, church should be all about Him, right?

Small little story, I was telling my grandfather about one of the churches I was serving at. There we had multiple services, four in total on the weekend, and every aspect of the services were planned out to the second. If the congregation really engaged in worship, I would motion to the band to repeat a verse or chorus in the moment. This after all was what I was instructed to do, bring powerful worship to each service. If the worship lasted over 18 minutes however, right on the second the pastor would come up on the stage, even in the middle of the song, acting like nothing was out of the ordinary. On several occasions, the worship band would immediately stop if the team was paying attention to something other than the song. A few times we encountered dreadful slow stopping point, like each band member fell asleep at different times or all the air slowly deflating out of a set of bagpipes. It was hard to plan for, always sudden, and didn't have an ounce of solid communication involved. The pastor would start speaking on the mic and the service would proceed to the announcement time. I used to call this, "Worship Whiplash" - you are moving along with the music, everything's fine and going great, and then out of nowhere an abrupt stop! My grandfather looked at me with a stern face and without hesitation said, "Wow, sounds like God couldn't get into that church with a crowbar!" His words still ring in my ears to this day.

Our God is one who plans.

I believe beyond a shadow of a doubt that before time began, God had a vision for our lives and saw you and me at this very instant. He knows everything before, every possibility of the present, and every future road that exists with all their variables, twists and turns. He clearly set the heavens and the Earth into motion a long time ago. I don't think He goes back to the drawing board every morning saying, "Ok, now how do you make this sunrise stuff happen again?" If He wants to, He can certainly change it up, but I believe He's planned out more than we could ever imagine. Because of who He is, and built within our being of the Imago Dei (Image of God), we then have the license and ability to plan as well. This means it's a good thing for us to build some plans, be intentional about what will happen in church.

Think about your songs. Here are some questions to ask yourself when building your plan.

1. Do you have a service theme? (Building a service around a theme can really help tie things together.)
2. How do the songs apply to the theme of the service?
    a. Do the song themes fit together individually and / or support the overarching theme of the service?
3. How do the songs work together?
    a. Are the songs leading you in a particular direction?
    b. Do the songs flow together according to the Key of the songs?
4. What is the Orchestration of the songs?
    a. Can you "perform" all songs with your available team?
    b. Are there specific solos that are needed to do a song well?
    c. Will you need to modify any songs because of needed solos, or the addition of other creative elements?

The Mark of a Powerful Rehearsal

- A System for Planning

1. Find a Creative and Effective way to Plan
2. "Creatives" and the Analytical side of the job
3. Online Service Planning
4. Our God is Present in the Moment.
5. Our God is one who plans.

CHAPTER 2:

ONE MAN BAND

We are better together.

We are designed to serve with one another.

1 Peter 4:10 "As each has received a gift, use it to serve one another, as good stewards of God's varied grace…"

I love thinking of worship ministry as a puzzle. Have you ever played with a Barrel of Monkeys? It's a very simple toy, which has always helped me understand church ministry.

Imagine with me, you open up this small yellow barrel, and these little red plastic monkeys spill out. Each little monkey figure has a smiling face, curled tail, and their arms create a hook on each side of their body. The object of the game is to pick up one monkey, and using its hand on one side, pick up another monkey from the pile by its other hand, feet, legs or whatever is available. Your goal is to connect all the monkeys together. Now that's an easy application to ministry, right? I could say a lot about most churches and parallel actions of primal animals living in the jungle, but I'll just move on.

I've always viewed our goal as ministry leaders as playing with a Barrel of Monkeys. It is our responsibility to look at all the pieces we have. Ask the question, "who has God brought together in our unique and specific church body?" Then we get to figure out how we can strategically connect everyone to God's vision and purpose. When we have everyone connected, I believe we get a better picture of what Heaven is going to look like.

Psalm 95:1 "Oh come, let us sing to the Lord; let us make a joyful noise to the rock of our salvation!"

The psalmist here is clearly inviting many people into the action of praise and worship. We can see here from scripture that inviting others into the act of worship incorporates more than just one person. Each of us has received a gift; let us sing to the Lord together!

Check out this incredible story from the book of Joshua.

Joshua 6:2-5 2 Then the Lord said to Joshua, "See, I have delivered Jericho into your hands, along with its king and its fighting men. 3 March around the city once with all the armed men. Do this for six days. 4 Have seven priests carry trumpets of rams' horns in front of the ark. On the seventh day, march around the city seven times, with the priests blowing the trumpets. 5 When you hear them sound a long blast on the trumpets, have the whole army give a loud shout; then the wall of the city will collapse and the army will go up, everyone straight in."

Talk about a worship team leading a congregation into a shout of praise! There were essentially 7 worship leaders here, playing and marching in front of an army. Can you imagine having a small but extended time of worship that spanned 7 days? What would the atmosphere be like? How would the people be praying and talking to one another? What would everyone be expecting and hoping to see? Feel free to present this idea to your congregation this weekend. "Hey everyone, we're going to worship, praise God, make a bunch of noise, and when I give you the cue... SHOUT like you mean it and watch God move!" Joshua's army sure saw God move, in a tangible way that literally brought down a massive stone building. You want to see God move in powerful ways? Get others to worship with you!

Delegate

I love playing different instruments. There's just something about feeling the freedom to move from one method of expression to another. If I'm leading a "fully-stocked" team with Keys, ELG, Bass, Drums, and tight Vocals, then there's nothing I like more than strapping on my Les Paul, using a windmill action with my arm to strum those power chords and feel the unbridled amplification in a band that is ready to Rock! For sets that are a little more reserved, I'll play an Acoustic guitar and be more than happy to drive the rhythm section with some steady strum patterns. For soft, intimate worship songs, I love to play the piano and focus on light melodies and motifs accentuated in the right hand. I have worked hard to learn several different instruments and become proficient enough to lead with confidence in many different styles. However, I have no desire to play every single note or lead every section.

As fun as it is for me to be able to play many different

instruments, it's important to remember there are other monkeys in this barrel and my job is not to be like a frantic sports superstar trying to cover every base. Can you just picture a World Series baseball team… filled by only one person? It would be hilarious and impossible to see one person pitching the ball, scrambling to the outfield for the catch, and then throwing the ball to himself all the way back at home plate for a triple play to win the game. Physically this can't be done and should never be attempted if you want to play well! There are many different positions in the game of baseball, each with their own purpose and relatively far distance between each other. The game is meant to be played by multiple people in order for it to look and function as the game of baseball. While we're on the subject, every sport has its own rules and purposes for each position. You are penalized if you have more than 11 players on the field in football, 5 players for basketball, 9 for baseball and I think you're getting the idea. Though these are just games, the objective for each team is to be unified towards a common goal.

My point here is for those leaders who are talented, and skilled in the ability to play many instruments and cover other parts, have some restraint. In every church I've served, I always give the same speech at some time or another. "This is not the Ken Jansen Show!" I understand that because I am called to be a leader, I will often have to step up and take the spotlight. But, if I am ever in the position solely for the spotlight and not to bring others to the presence of God in an act of service, then my motives may not be in the right place and I need to reset my alignment to serve.

There are many others in the church who have been gifted to play the same instruments I can. They may even be better than I am in a particular way. The best thing I could do to lead a team well, would be to discover each person's gifting. This can easily be done by a thorough audition or close observation over several rehearsals and services. I then place east person in different positions and look to see what the best arrangement is for a unified and strongest possible team configuration. I don't suggest trying to do this for a large team all at once, rather spread out your observations and auditions over a period of time where you can give more attention to each person's skill set.

Who's in Your Band?

Make sure in the planning stages of your rehearsal, you are mindful of everyone on your team. Do you have a team member who is really strong on an instrument? Why not pick out some parts for that person to play, specifically giving them an area to shine in using their gift? There are many contemporary worship songs that have great guitar solos. Look no further than Lincoln Brewster and you'll get an idea of what I'm talking about.

Romans 12:6-8 (NLT) "In his grace, God has given us different gifts for doing certain things well."

Remember that each person's gift has been given by God.

James 1:17 (NIV) "Every good and perfect gift is from above, coming down from the Father of the heavenly lights..."

I'm sure I'm not the only one who has ever been uncomfortable with receiving a complement directed towards me, when it really should have been said for the whole team (especially after a dynamic and moving service). This is not uncommon for worship leaders and artists. It's an area I struggled with in my first several years of leadership. I always felt that complements aimed towards me as a leader, which reflected the gifts and contributions of others, should be directed towards God and the whole group instead. I was very hesitant in receiving praise about great music and performances. I heard a wise speaker discuss this very topic and realized that I was denying someone from using their gift of encouragement. By not receiving their words, I was in turn denying the very gift God had given to them intended for me to receive.

Now back to the musical context, you may be on the fence about the use of solos in corporate worship. Years ago, I was overly cautious about using solos. I didn't want people in the congregation to be distracted, with nothing to sing, looking up at the stage as the lights and all attention were now on an individual instead of eyes drifting in some other, more Holy direction. I realized though, after a lot of prayer, reflection, questioning and challenges to my worship department, that we could encourage the whole church to celebrate the great things God has done by allowing someone to shine with the amazing gift they'd been given. Let those Electric Guitar solos fly, let that Soprano belt out the latest Kari Jobe lead line, and let the drummer go nuts like Animal from the Muppets in the intro… as long as the glory can be pointed back to God, you can help everyone see another side of who God is - The Giver of All Good Things!

The Mark of a Powerful Rehearsal

- One Man Band

1. We are better together.
2. Delegate
3. Who's in Your Band?

CHAPTER 3:

CLICK TRACKS

Why Use Click Tracks?

This question could spark a much longer conversation than what we'll go into here. For the purpose of this book, we'll talk about using click tracks to augment your current band situation. If you have never used click tracks, they are simply recordings you play along with which include, at the very least, a sounded metronome marking. You can build upon this metronome (the click) to include vocal cues to direct the band, and other recorded instruments. I have worked with many bands and churches without clicks, and also worked with many that use tracks exclusively. The benefits and drawbacks vary. Personally, I love the freedom of being fluid throughout a set, repeating sections or stopping for an unplanned pause if the spirit leads... but I also like having a structure that is clear and easy to follow with my team. If you are looking for more information on starting to use Click Tracks, how to do it successfully, and what you'll need as far as equipment, check out Downpourintl.com for a full list that'll work for varying budgets.

Produce Your Own

I am blessed to be able to produce my own Click Tracks for the different teams I work with. As an artist with a passion for the process and end product, I like being able to build a song set to go along with the vision God has given me for the service. This creation control includes instrumentation, order of Verse / Chorus / Repeats /

Solos included or excluded.

Avid's ProTools is fantastic software and pretty much the recording industry's standard when it comes to fully produced music. It allows endless possibilities in creating, recording, and building tracks for live performance. This software has a bit of a learning curve, but once you get the hang of it, and understand the location of different tools, it has a lot of similarities to other DAW's (Digital Audio Workstation) and I find it to be the most powerful, least inhibiting, and best at executing exactly what I'm looking for.

Below is a screenshot of one of my songs built off the template I've compiled.

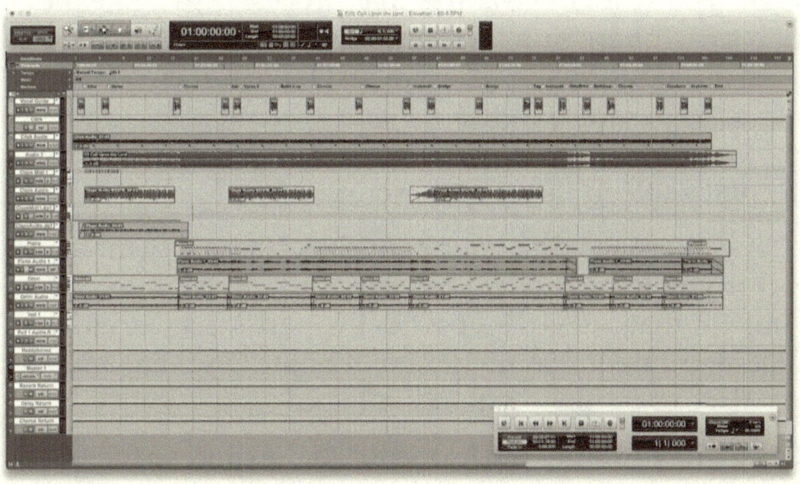

When I create my clicks, I start off with a custom saved template I created. This has several preset instruments I've compiled that pretty much cover the full gamut of most worship songs and contemporary songs in general. I import the song mp3 I'm looking to cover into a new track and then work to find the correct tempo so I can build everything to sync up with the original song. I then record my actual Click, using a wood block plugin / sound with just a touch of reverb for a realistic tone. I add in my vocal cues for different sections by listening to the song and adding markers where the cues will begin, making sure they are timed to the precise beat of action and section change. From there I go about adding in the different instruments needed to augment the band I'll be performing with. Often times I'll just start out with a simple Pad to add some "glue" before adding the other elements. Most of your contemporary worship songs will have some amount of Pad in them anyway, so you're pretty safe to add an amount of ambient tones to hold the piece together, fill in the crack (use your own term - however you want to visualize that process). Just like they used to say, "There's always room for Jell-O!" After the song starts taking shape, you can just have full creative license as to different Guitar / Piano / Synth solos you want to add in, throw in some iconic musical motifs that are recognizable in the original song.

***If you are making your own click tracks, I want to stress for you to have some fun with this. Even if no one else notices that little extra part in the performance, maybe a small instrumental motif, you will know it's there and it adds a flare of originality that is all you!

Once I have all my tracks recorded, I export each one and load them into the next software platform I use, which is Ableton Live, another fantastic program. Some people use this program as their sole DAW and they build incredibly complex audio / midi compositions. You've got the option with Ableton to have unending variations in midi instrument creation and sound manipulation. You can directly record audio with it, building songs in varying different modes or visual methods of creation. You can choose a linear / more traditional recording view, or record in small blocks of armed tracks.

Here's a picture of my Ableton Live template for keeping my tracks organized. I've setup vertical rows for each instrument, some rows including multiple possible instruments in one. I can then go into each instrument and mute that channel or make selections based on my available team for that service. This makes using tracks incredibly easy as you can customize the orchestration anytime you like in a live setting.

I use Ableton mainly to "Fire / Launch" my tracks. The learning curve with this program is a bit challenging at first, just because there are so many different options and it's arranged differently from many other traditionally DAW user interfaces, but once you get the hang of it, the tools are very simple to understand. You can be a novice and still build some great sets to use in a service. I've seen others who are self-declared experts with Ableton do some really incredible stuff. I spent quite a lot of time and effort building my template for use in live Worship. I wanted to have something that would be easy to use, easy to keep organized for weeks and years to come, and also powerful in execution to help me and my teams shine on the weekend and when working with other churches.

Feel free to check out my resources page on Downpourintl.com to learn more about Ableton templates and to jumpstart your journey in using Click Tracks. You can even download the template I use to start firing your own clicks this weekend!

Click Track Resources

There are many different services out there providing bands with Click Tracks. It's very rare for me to see a large church or touring band that isn't using in-ear monitors and playing to a click. Nowadays, for the nominal price of "X-amount" of dollars, you too can sing along with the same Guitar that's accompanying Chris Tomlin on his latest album! If that's not the artist you're looking to emulate, checking different resources will open up a world of other possibilities. I've used a few different services to buy tracks from, the main ones being Loopcommunity.com and Multitracks.com.

When I first ventured into using clicks for worship, my church's budget was not arranged for consistent music purchases and I wasn't creating my own at that point. I found LoopCommunity and it really was a game changer. It's a great service and like the name says, it really is a community of other artists. You're able to find profiles of worship pastors, guitarists, light engineers and people who just play music as a hobby. These artists are regular people like you and me who've created some great music for their own church bands. They've uploaded their tracks to

LoopCommunity, and for varying purchase prices, you can download stems (individual instrument recorded files) used by their church and others around the world. The prices of the tracks have different ranges, depending on what software platform you'd like to use it for and the quality of the stems (wav vs. mp3). You also have the ability to become one of their contributors, which is a great way to make a little extra money and help other churches and bands benefit from your hard work. They take care of all the licensing for the songs and recordings, which is a huge bonus!

After using LC for a while, I started looking for some tracks that were more like the original recordings. I then found the next resource that was like striking gold. MultiTracks.com is a fantastic site that has tons of different recorded stems from the actual artist. As I was saying before, you can actually play along with Tomlin's guitar, Israel Houghton's rhythm section, or Lincoln Brewster's ELG solos! Downloading tracks off this site are generally more expensive. Depending on your budget, you may not be able to do it all the time, but I would recommend picking out a few songs that your church is really passionate about. Maybe there's an anthem for your church, one that brings everyone together when it's sung. I would recommend to spend a little extra money to get some super high-quality band reinforcement. This anthem will probably be used several times in the future, so you can look at this purchase as an investment into great sound for years to come.

I've had many sets where I purchased one powerful track for the first song from MultiTracks.com for a song I really wanted to come off in a certain way. The next song I then had a track from LoopCommunity that incorporated some great recorded parts but maybe not as many as the first track. The last songs in my set had just some simple tracks incorporating only click and pads, maybe some light piano. I had a variation of band reinforcement for the set from full-on to a light backing. It sounded great with variation in dynamics, instrumentation and drive from a full sound towards our more intimate worship time.

I hope this helps you think about manageable solutions if you're looking to get into using tracks. You don't have to go in 100% or expect to pay a ton to get rolling.

Really quick, I know I mentioned Ableton Live as my preferred launching software, but beginners in this area can use anything with the ability to build a playlist; iTunes, Windows Media Player, an iPod / iPhone, computer or tablet.

The Mark of a Powerful Rehearsal

- Click Tracks

1. Produce Your Own
2. Click Track Resources

CHAPTER 4:

PRACTICE BY YOURSELF

I cannot stress enough how important it is for you to prepare. Hopefully you understand by this point in the book, preparation is an essential element in building a Powerful Rehearsal. If you are planning your set in advance, sending out communication, building a culture around excellence and asking others to come to rehearsal with their part prepared as well, then you definitely need to practice!

Whether you are reading this book as a team leader, or you're typically playing an instrument or singing on the team, you need to know your part. I've never had any verbal altercations with anyone on my teams about this, but I have had to extensively teach the difference between "Practice" and "Rehearsal."

Practice - what you do on your own, learning your notes, how to finger certain chords on the piano / guitar, learning rhythms and preparing your part **Before** joining the team in rehearsal.

Rehearsal - the time when everyone comes together, adds their individual parts and preparation to create a symphony of unified sound. Instruction should be provided on collective ideals such as dynamics, transitions, giving space for other instruments and shaping the overall performance.

When you're leading and building a Powerful Rehearsal, you need individual practice time. This will give you a better understanding of how your part will direct and guide others not only in the rehearsal, but in the congregational worship service as well. During your personal practice time, pay attention to what part you are playing. Your mind may want to listen to the songs as a whole and start thinking about how the rest of the band will sound, how one of your team members will need to practice their part extra hard. Do not lose focus on You! This needs to be a time when you can relax, forget about the stresses of leadership, and work on your own craft. God has gifted you in an amazing way and it is your own responsibility to use and develop that gift.

I will often practice in front of my computer. I setup my guitar and pedalboard, cue my songs to practice, and put each song on repeat until I have the part down. I'll play along with the recording a few times while making note of where I need to stop playing or mark in my music specific sections to remember including solos and unique instrumental lines. Then I stop the song after each challenging spot, and just rewind the section till I get it and can move on. I've toyed around with using my recording software to make small clips of solos or parts I want to continually go over, but I often find that creates a lot more work for me to do before I even get to the practice portion. Remember to just stay focused and get those parts down through repetition and improving your technique.

When you feel you have spent a sufficient amount of time on your part and you are comfortable playing it forwards and backwards, then and only then should you start looking at the needs for the rest of the band. You'll be amazed at how much more you listen to things going on around you when you don't have to pay attention so much to your own part. With your part memorized and learned to a level of proficiency, you'll also be much better at guiding others in their respective parts. You'll feel the freedom to put your instrument or mic down, take a small pause in rehearsal, and give some one-on-one encouragement or coaching to another band member who may be struggling with their part.

Continuing with your personal practice time, now ask yourself a few questions.

1. What are the solos doing in the song?
2. Where do the solos enter / drop out?
3. Do I know the rhythm of the lead lines?
4. Do I know all the words?
5. Do I understand and feel comfortable explaining the dynamic changes?
6. What are some key elements in this song that make it unique and how can I describe these to the band?

Answering each of these questions give you what I call, "The Director's Edge." You see the song as a full work of art. You see the in's and out's, the up's and down's. Instead of looking at a white piece of paper with black symbols on it, you see a vibrant painting with colors that change from one song to the next. The more you understand the song, the greater you'll be able to Direct your band from a rough finger painting to a masterpiece Da Vinci.

Having this full understanding of the song and how all the parts come together will give you a clear picture of what is needed from the rest of your team during rehearsal. Remember the vision you started with for the service? You want to keep that vision in mind and keep building different pillars to help support the platform of the end result.

The Mark of a Powerful Rehearsal

– Practice By Yourself

1. Individual Practice
2. Corporate Rehearsal

CHAPTER 5:

BUILD YOUR SYLLABUS

In the same way a teacher develops a curriculum before the start of the school year, you need to build a game plan for how you want your rehearsal time to play out. Maybe you've heard the old adage, "If you fail to plan, you plan to fail." I don't like the world "fail," but I understand that you will not achieve the results you are hoping for if planning has not been an integral stage in developing your rehearsal.

Dreams of being a Rock Star

If we look for some wisdom in scripture about planning ahead, Proverbs has a ton of encouragement. I encourage you to take this verse to heart.

Proverbs 16:3 *(ESV) Commit your work to the Lord, and your plans will be established.*

Commit this service to the Lord without delay. Right from the beginning of your planning stages, pray and work to understand the vision for this service. I imagine you are talented, gifted, artistic and skilled in many things, but remember this service is not about You or me! We have to point everything back to God. When we hand over the glorification to Him alone, we enter into an amazing and harmonious relationship where He does more through us than we could ever hope to do on our own. God will establish your plans and bring them together in a way that is clear and effective to everyone on your team.

It's funny that just a few verses later in Proverbs we

find,

Proverbs 16:9 *(ESV) The heart of man plans his way, but the Lord establishes his steps.*

I look at this verse and laugh in spite of myself. There have been countless times where I wanted to make my own plans, believing they were beneficial to the Kingdom of God, but truly they originated from an inner desire to see something come about that I personally wanted. I remember early in my Worship Leading career, I was learning more about the particular skill of "Picking out Songs" for use in a corporate worship service. I had been listening to one of my favorite bands at the time, Jars of Clay, and their song "I Need You" was resonating with my heart. I would listen to it over and over again on repeat, singing out each word and memorizing the band dynamics. I felt a strong desire to use this song in a worship service in the hopes that it would move others the same way it did for me. I prepared the charts, the rehearsal, the slides for use on the screens and when the time came to sing the song in the service… I slowly felt all my hope and excitement leave as I saw a crowd motionless. They didn't seem to be singing, no one clapped on the beat during the song or after it finished, and the energy seemed to run out of the room like a pool which had sprung a leak. How could they not be moved by this song that so easily got me pumped up to sing about how I need Jesus?

I can now look back at that service and smile as there were many other contributing factors that most likely led to the lack of enthusiasm from others. Some of those factors were that the song was new, I probably could've introduced it better, this particular congregation enjoyed a style of music that was a little different than Jars of Clay, and the song may not have fit well with the other songs in the set. I immediately learned a valuable lesson I've taken with me from that day,

"Leading others into worship, picking out songs, singing and playing with a band is not about me, it's about getting in touch with what God is doing and wants to do in the hearts of those in my church."

I know that I had the best intentions in picking out that song. I truly wanted others to be moved by it as much as I was. But, I also saw within my heart the desire to be on stage with Dan Haseltine, lead singer of Jars of Clay, and have the band backing me up. If you're an artist and admire other musicians, you've probably had some experience imagining yourself in the shoes of your favorite band members, wondering what it would be like… We have to lay that down and seek after the calling God has given us. Your calling may be to form a band and travel the world, playing huge venues for all your fans. If so, that's great. However, if you're called to be a Worship Leader, pray and determine where your boundaries are so you are not confused on your calling. Understand limits so you won't be asking more of yourself, your band, or your congregation. If you think your church should behave like those in an auditorium of screaming Beatles fans and your band should be able to play hits from Rush without hesitation, you may want to revisit your expectations and support your band and church as to what God has called them to be.

How long should a rehearsal last?

I've had rehearsals that only last 15 minutes in dire circumstances, and I've led others that lasted several hours for a large production. Making a plan for your rehearsal, no matter how long, is crucial to achieve your goals. Use discretion in how long you can push your team to stay engaged and focused, and how much time you need to cover all needed areas in musical instruction to perform the set well.

I recommend a weekly two-hour time slot for most teams and churches. If you can't get the songs rehearsed in two hours, maybe you should reevaluate having those songs in your weekend plan. If your rehearsal is under two hours you run the risk of not having ample time to go over important and challenging sections. Also, your teammates may not find it "worth coming to" especially if they have to drive a long distance. For example: a person driving 45 minutes to setup and rehearse for 30 minutes, then to tear down and drive back home would equal 1.5 hours of driving for only 30 mins of rehearsal time. You can always let your team go home early after having achieved all of your Syllabus goals.

* Leadership Tip - volunteers always like hearing they're being let go early.

What is A Syllabus? – An Outline

A Syllabus is just an outline of the subjects in a course of study or teaching. So, when you're building the plan for your rehearsal, assemble an outline of what you want to go over and accomplish. This can be digital by use of Planning Center Online, a Word document, a text message, or by use of a bunch sticky notes on a cork board. Whatever method you choose, make sure it's something you're comfortable using and will help you keep organized records for the next steps and future service planning.

So, let's build your Syllabus! At this point you want to recall the important elements in all the songs you've practiced in your individual time. This syllabus can be as easy as your song list order. At this point I start making notes of some challenging rhythm sections and areas where I want some specific dynamic contrasts. When you become more accustomed to thinking about your rehearsal in this way, you'll automatically remember the different sections and what is needed to rehearse them, so you'll only need a light guide to remember what comes next. Below is a simple syllabus to serve as a guide.

Simple Rehearsal Syllabus

A. Opening / Rehearsal Rundown
B. Song 1
C. Song 2
D. Song 3
E. Song 4
F. Going Back
G. Transitions

To take this Syllabus to another level, let's expand it to reflect some different sections into challenge points and important areas you really want to go over in rehearsal. Here's an example of an expanded syllabus from one of my rehearsals.

Expanded Rehearsal Syllabus

A. **Opening** – Quick Prayer asking God to bless the rehearsal time

1. Start playing the first song at the beginning of rehearsal – Right On Time / when it's supposed to start – 6:00 PM sharp!
2. Welcome Everyone
3. Ask if everyone was able to Practice the songs before rehearsal

4. If someone says No, then you know right away to bring up and address their specific instrument / solo areas in each song.
5. ***Do not leave this up to chance that they'll magically just "get their part!"
6. Discuss the Order of the songs

B. Song 1

1. Make note of the tempo and the "Feel" of the song
2. ELG Solos / Drum Riffs
3. Breakdown section with only drums, vocals continue, everyone claps their hands to get the congregation engaged

C. Song 2

1. Changing who has the solos
2. Possible focus change from ELG to Piano for example
3. Continue to keep the energy up

D. Song 3

1. Focus on areas where Band gives more space for Vocals to come out more

E. Song 4

1. Begin song softly, build in intensity, dies down at the end to same dynamics as beginning

F. Going Back

1. Go back through the set to rework problem areas

G. Transitions

1. Make multiple run-throughs ending one song and beginning next
2. Discuss the Worship Momentum / Inertia of the set with the band

The Mark of a Powerful Rehearsal

- Build Your Syllabus

1. How long should a rehearsal last?
2. What is A Syllabus? - An Outline
3. Simple Rehearsal Syllabus
4. Expanded Rehearsal Syllabus

CHAPTER 6:

SET THE STAGE

Please don't take this in a selfish way, but I always start with my area first when setting up the stage for rehearsal. I confidently coach myself as I start putting things together,

"Get your own gear Right!"

Think of it as flying on a plane and hearing the stewardess tell you during the safety protocols, "Put on your own mask before helping to put a mask on the person next to you." You are preparing for trouble up ahead. You will encounter some turbulence in this rehearsal going over challenging parts and working with different caliber artists.

You will feel so much better when your gear is setup to the point where you can comfortably perform your best. You can relax, knowing that when you come to play your instrument or sing in your spot, all of your equipment is ready to go. If you've got your pedal board, instrument, or a microphone setup just the way you like it, the rest of your time in rehearsal can be dedicated to the health and training of others. You're now free to move on to creating an environment that is welcoming and encouraging to the rest of your team.

I can't count how many rehearsals I've been to, where I was not the leader but playing a supporting role, and was not given the opportunity to fully setup and test my equipment. I've arrived in plenty of time to plug in my instrument etc., but then no consideration has been given for me to speak with the sound tech or stage manager to check my own levels. This may happen because of a leader that is unsure of the needs for each instrument, or it's possible the leader doesn't have high enough standards for being prepared themselves. I don't want this to sound like I am tearing down other leaders, but we must have high standards when preparing to lead others into God's presence. Every time I have been responsible for my own setup, I make sure to arrive early to give more than enough time to prepare all of my gear. That often means leaving the house early, thinking ahead about dealing with traffic, the time and effort for unloading my car, and setting up on the stage far in advance before the rehearsal is scheduled to start.

I feel stressed when I am not given the opportunity to go through my own little sound check before the start of rehearsal. I need a few minutes to make sure my instrument is setup properly, things are hooked up in the right order and I'm able to produce the tone I've worked so hard for. Without that time, I'm unsure about how my instrument is setup. I need to hear myself play or sing in the environment to determine what I'll be mindful of during the rehearsal. Without this environmental status check, I don't know how I will sound through the PA system. I'm starting off on the wrong foot with a lack of confidence. I'll be shy about singing or playing out because I know the rest of the band will hear me when I can't even tell how I sound. If I sound bad, I don't want to be a poor reflection of my gift. I certainly don't want to distract anyone else from giving his or her best. Having a proper amount of time to setup allows me to give my absolute best. Denying anyone else the opportunity of giving their best is wrong and should be avoided at all cost.

Imagine you are an Olympic athlete, waiting patiently in the dark hallway tunnel underneath the stadium seats. In a moment, you will step out from the tunnel into the light, and within seconds start your race. You have no idea if the sun is shining, or possibly the skies are pouring down rain. You are also not aware of the track you'll be running on. Will be racing on asphalt, grass, dirt, or soupy mud? Put yourself into those shoes and think about all the different ways you would prepare for the changes in environment. The same thoughts can be taken for musicians playing in a large church with padded seats, a small church with wooden floors and a vaulted ceiling, or a portable stage assembled in the middle of high-school gym. You need to prepare your gear for your environment.

Servant Leadership

Servant Leadership is highly important in all areas of life for a Christ follower. In regards to being a Worship Leader / Pastor, it will help to win over the most challenging of team members and situations. When you seek to bring others together from various backgrounds, different church experiences, and unequal levels of musical instruction and skill, you will understand ministry in a new way as you prepare a place for each of your team members.

I've been blessed to serve with guys who are recording artists and have been playing "the professional circuit" for more years than I've been alive. I've worked with vocalists that could blow the roof off Carnegie Hall. I've incorporated young kids at the middle school age and mentored them through their high-school years to become foundational members of the church's Worship Department. With extremely varying skill levels, I've found success in building a cohesive group by seeking to welcome each person in a unique way to the team, the rehearsal and the weekend worship experience.

This is such a huge part of ministry that sadly many pastors overlook. It becomes a lot of fun building relationships with individual team members.

- Invest in each person.
- Get to know their interests.
- Find out what gets them excited, particularly when it comes to music.
- Make it a point to provide encouragement in your rehearsal in regards to each person's interests.

This is a huge portion of your leadership acumen. So, make sure you are paying attention here! You are in charge of creating an environment for the entire church during your worship service, but you are also creating a meaningful and welcoming environment for each person on your team. You are a servant by taking your vested interest in them and giving it life. We'll go over a few things you can do in the next sections. The more you serve in this manner, you show others the importance of interest on an individual level. Model the behavior you wish others to follow. This is one of the most powerful leadership tools to promote your vision.

On numerous occasions, I have played or sung at different churches to help fill out their team. I'm thankful for the opportunity to do so, but I'm often disappointed in the circumstance of being the "new person on the team." I may get a couple people asking who I am, or thanking me for singing / playing, but rarely do I have conversations that serve to build a new relationship. We are part of the same "family." 2 Corinthians 6:18 says that we are sons and daughters of the Lord Almighty. We need to build relationships to further the Kingdom of God. Don't ever forget this! Whether you are welcoming a new face in the pews, or a familiar one who has served on the worship team for a few years, invest in building a relationship. This relationship can be vitally important in the life of another, and will strengthen your leadership skills as well.

The Stage has Zones

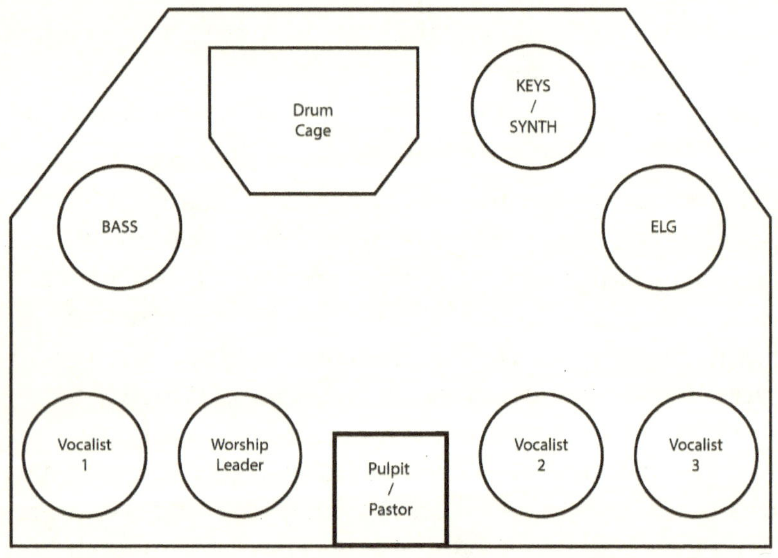

I like to think of the stage as having "Zones" where individual musicians will operate. This gives each person an area they can call his or her own, move around, and have a space in which to setup their own gear. Psychologically, when you tell someone where they will be singing / playing, this gives them a sense of direction and a feeling that they fit in. I always feel more comfortable when I know where I'm supposed to be. Ever shown up for a party at a stranger's house, walked through the door, and you didn't know where to go or where you belonged?

... Same idea here. This may be something small, but it adds to the overall impression to your team how you've crafted and planned for this rehearsal.

By looking at this graphic, you can see how setting up a stage can quickly become complex for a team comprising of 8 members. You'll need music stands for everyone, unless Vocalist 2 and 3 want to share (which I generally discourage as I want ask each person to make notes in their own music). Assuming you have 3 Vocalists as well as your Worship Leader, you're looking at setting up 5 mics altogether, including the Pastor's mic. Then you have a line and DI box for each instrument and a host of mics for an acoustic drum set. You'll also need to determine your stage monitor arrangement and setup, in-ears or wedges. Maybe you have a larger or smaller team, but I hope you can see how it's easy to spend a good amount of time making sure each musician is setup properly and all lines are correctly connected to your sound system.

Preparing a stage like this can be more labor intensive if and when you change your stage decorations, add or subtract musicians, or have a Lead Pastor that openly embraces OCD tendencies regarding "clutter on the stage." If you have time to setup the stage on a day other than rehearsal day, I suggest doing it then. This will give you time to stay focused solely on the musical needs before rehearsal.

* Leadership Tip - setting the stage can be a great opportunity to involve new Sound Tech volunteers and team members. You can quickly build into your leaders and new volunteers by teaching how to setup the stage, explaining the sound system, and spending time connecting relationally while doing manual intensive tasks like moving staging or a heavy grand piano.

Prepare a place for your team.

If you know that one of your team members has a bad back, setup their favorite chair for rehearsal so they are comfortable and still able to play. If another person needs help to setup an in-ear monitor mix, take some extra time to build / save / and setup their mix for them before they plug in. Plan on taking some extra time to get things prepared not just for you, but also for everyone on your team. Even if that means arriving one to two hours early, you will reap relational and performance benefits you previously didn't think possible. Your team will notice the extra effort, even if it's small, and that could mean the difference between encouraging them to worship with all they've got and seeing a team member give up thinking they don't matter.

I've had members on my worship team who were not able stand for a full two-hour rehearsal. I let them try every stool with back support / no back support, any chair I could find and all the benches the church had on hand until they found one they thought was the most comfortable. I was looking for whichever chair would help them be able to serve their best during rehearsal. Every time I had that person on my team, I pictured in my mind the stage setup and their favorite chair was associated with the place I would prepare for them.

I had an elderly man on one of my teams that had a prosthetic leg from the knee down. He was awesome. I still laugh when I think about him. He used to crack me up by sitting in the chair I prepared for him, and during times I was rehearsing others in the band, he would swing his prostheses around in a circle like a propeller. Was it a little distracting? Yes! But, it was always great comic relief.

The team members appreciated how I thought of them even before the rehearsal started. I built relationships with each one of them and care about their experience in the rehearsal. You can do little things like setting up a chair, placing organized music on everyone's stands, or even giving a small gift like a new recording or album to someone who may be interested. I would sometimes bring in food or snacks to celebrate a team members birthday. I made sure not to detract from our rehearsal time and the need to prepare for the service, but would do my best to end early and give time for fellowship and connection with others at the end.

The Mark of a Powerful Rehearsal

- Set The Stage

1. "Get your own gear Right!"
2. Servant Leadership
3. The Stage has Zones
4. Prepare a place for your team

CHAPTER 7:
START THE CLOCK

Effectively Communicate the Start Time of rehearsal to everyone involved.

If you're using a service like PCO, then make sure all of your email reminders with dates, times for services and rehearsals are correct. You can setup templates using PCO that will automatically take care of this weekly communication. You can easily setup this kind of automation to even send notices to cell phones via text message.

Make sure you start the rehearsal ON TIME!

I had a teacher that used to say, "You can never be on time. You're either Early… or Late." Even if team members are still walking through the door or setting up their gear, make sure you start the first song in your Syllabus right as the clock hits the time you communicated. This will give everyone a sense of importance and urgency to be ready on time or they will miss their part. Everyone else who is on time will understand the commitment. Would you feel comfortable knowing everyone is playing while you're still unpacking your instrument or walking through the door? That kind of makes you stick out like a sore thumb, doesn't it?

Enforce the standards after they are set.

Text your team if they are late. This may make you seem like the bad guy / gal, but you need to let your team members know the standard you have set, the standard applies to everyone, and EACH person is important to the plan. You cannot over-communicate the importance for each person to be at rehearsal early, that every position matters, and you miss them when they are not there.

Make audible notice of people who are late.

I have never gotten excited about confrontations; I don't know anyone who has. This may be challenging for you. When someone is walking in late, and especially if they are not running to setup their gear, I'll make mention of the situation on the microphone so everyone can hear.

"Hey (for example: Matthew / Sarah), there he / she is! Come on, let's go! We started at 6:00 (Insert start time here)!"

Comments like this, made in specific to the person being late, but also in the presence of the whole team, can take the sting out of a personal attack or any implication of trying to make that one person feel bad. You're not telling everyone you're angry at that person, or fostering an environment of looking down upon anyone, but you're enforcing the standards and communicating them again for the whole team. Once you call out this person, just move on to the rest of the rehearsal. You've got a lot to do from here!

Keep track of the time.

After you have started the rehearsal, keep track of what time it is throughout the rehearsal. This gives you an idea of how much time you're spending on different areas of the syllabus. Let's break this down into an equation.

If you spend more than 38 minutes on one song and you're planning to give each song the same attention, you've got a two-hour rehearsal, and 5 songs to prepare for the service, a little bit of math will reveal that you're not going to get done in the allotted time. You would instead be looking at rehearsing for over 3 hours.

I use my iPad in worship, using the app OnSong to keep track of all my lead charts and chord charts. One of the great features of using this tool in rehearsals and performances is that I get to see what time it is at the top of the screen. You can also achieve this by simply setting a smartphone on your stand, have a clock on the wall, use an old-fashioned wrist-watch, or hire your local Town Cryer to yell out the time every 15 minutes.

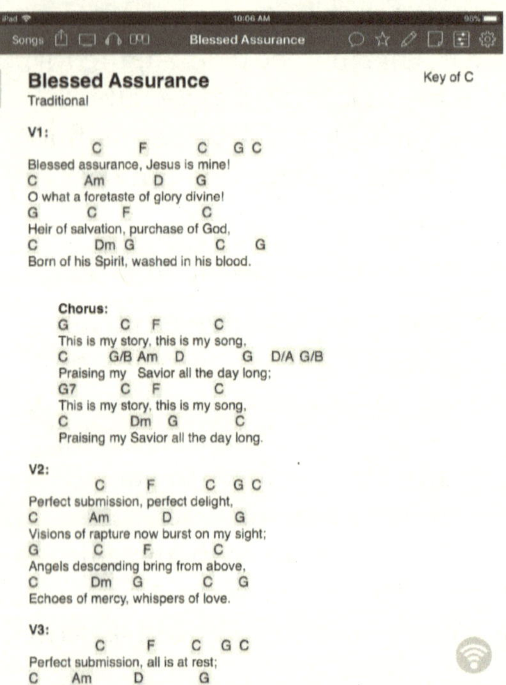

Be Mindful of Everyone's Time.

You want to respect everyone's time on your team. They are graciously giving you their weeknight / early morning / afternoon. They could've driven a long distance, had a terrible day at work before rehearsal, or they've got a husband or wife with 3 screaming kids that can't wait for them to get home and help! The point is that you don't know the full weight of what your team members are giving up to serve on your team. Take this gift from your team with graciousness and treat it as a prized possession. Honor their gift and seek to bless them in return.

I read a small book years ago by Andy Stanley called Choosing to Cheat. It's a fantastic little read that took me less than an hour, I recommend it. The main point of the book was about the decisions we make. Try not to get hung up on the word, "Cheat," as it can carry some heavy and negative connotations for some. Stanley argues that whatever we choose to do with our time, we are choosing to cheat someone or something else out of our time. If you choose to play a pickup basketball game with the guys tonight, you are choosing to cheat your wife and kids out of time you could be spending with them. If you choose to spend 15 extra hours on work this week, you may have to cheat yourself out of that rejuvenating hike or walk at the park, your ability to do house chores, or taking time to call your mom like you've been promising for weeks now. You get the picture. Don't feel bad about spending your time on something, just know that our decisions are important.

Steve Caswell has been my life coach for several years. He does wonders in helping me to change my perspective and focus my energy to where God would have me being most effective. The vocabulary we use is affects our thoughts and performance in life in a huge way. The words we use to describe our day, the actions we take, and the situations we are in directly impact the outcome of how we experience life and achieve our goals. I desire to perform at a high level. I want to succeed in accomplishing the tasks God has given me. I recognize that for me to succeed in the areas I'm passionate about, I need to encourage myself and keep stoking the fire to drive to the finish line. It's not hard for me to find my own buttons to push to bring myself down. My faults are readily accessible in my own mind. I can quickly get overwhelmed by thinking of all the tasks I spend my time on that I'm not passionate about.

Here's where Steve shares his gifting with me and flips the script to my thought process. He helped me to stop saying,

"I spend my time on this / that..."

I would frequently repeat these words, recounting how I'm tied up with areas that tear me down instead of building me up. When I mentally focus on jobs I don't necessarily care about, spending money to pay bills, trying to keep things afloat by repetitious tasks, I feel like the life is draining out of me. What if we describe these actions in another way?

1. Working different jobs allow me to **Develop new Skill Sets**.
2. Paying bills allow me to **Become a Wise Financier**.
3. Keeping things afloat teaches me to **Increase My Performance Abilities with Multiple Plates Spinning**.

I have changed my mindset. Instead of saying, "I spend," now I say,

"I'm INVESTING my time on this / that..."

Investing sounds a lot better, doesn't it? When you INVEST your time, you are giving importance and a stronger purpose to your task. Your team members are investing their time to serve on your team. Don't take that action lightly!

Prepare a Rehearsal full of Substance

Make sure you give your team an efficient amount of substance in the rehearsal. You want to have all your ducks in a row, know what's going to happen and be ready to lead your team to what needs to be accomplished next. If people show up and you're not prepared, you really don't know the parts that are needed to successfully perform the songs, or you're not giving any instruction to the team, they will sense this lack of preparation. You will either lose control of the rehearsal or you'll be creating a culture where people don't care about the standards you are attempting to set.

Carefully craft your steps according to the syllabus we described in chapter 6. There may be points you want to expand upon or revise and that's fine. This rehearsal is all about your vision and your specific team. Just be aware that you don't want to have such an easygoing rehearsal that your team doesn't feel like they got much accomplished. Go over parts multiple times. Try them in different arrangements. Try challenging points with different tempos - slow at first then up to tempo. Give time to address questions. If there are no questions, play the role of a musician on your team, maybe a newcomer, and imagine what question they may have. Put yourself in their shoes and answer a question they may have but may be too shy to ask. Thinking ahead and fully diving into the needs of your team members will set you apart as a leader. This makes the difference between, "trying to lead" and "directing" a rehearsal.

Don't Waste Time - Be Purposeful!

If there's one thing I see with inexperienced team leaders and conductors, it's wasting time on something that does not serve the vision. Let me be clear here, I love to talk and build relationships. I learned a long time ago, *"It's better to lead out of relationship than position."* I tell jokes all the time, I make fun of myself, I bring up quick stories of me going to the store or recalling a funny movie scene and ask if anyone else has seen it. When I do this, I am sensing there is a moment when I could help build up some relationship and trust with my team members. This is most often a split-second decision. I may be in the middle of a rehearsal, really pushing the team hard to go over a section for the 8th time. If I see the look of annoyance and a few people getting bored, I'll break the tension in that moment with a quick anecdote to get a chuckle, remind people we can have fun in rehearsal, then get back to the work at hand. This gives the team more of a connection with me as the leader, gives their mind a little study break, and helps re-energize them to get through that tough spot.

A couple examples of wasting time would be;

1. Telling a story that lasts more than a few minutes. By more than a few minutes, I'm talking more than 3 to 5. If you have a quick anecdote that lasts a couple minutes, and you get to the point, you're fine. If you go over a couple minutes, then you should really start wrapping it up. Going over 3 to 5 minutes means you've stopped rehearsal and now you're just hanging out. This isn't conversation time, it's rehearsal time.

2. Giving metaphors for how you want the song to sound, that don't make sense and do more to confuse everyone than lead them to being on the same page.

"In this section, I want the drums to sound like a train. A blue train traveling to upstate New York. The same train I rode on to see my parents for Christmas back when I was in college. I

didn't have enough money for a plane ticket, but that's ok because the airport in my home town smells like feet. Who knows why anyone would fly in there. Out of there? Absolutely! But, Christmas that year was a disaster, I only got one thing I'd hoped for and didn't spend anytime studying for finals. So, yeah… Ok, Drums 2, 3, 4!"

Scratching your head? Me too, that story didn't make a lick of sense. I have been in rehearsals with leaders that say stuff like this and it drives me crazy. All the energy that was driving towards learning the parts and bringing the song together, I can feel it leave the room. I just want to shout out, "I love ya, but Get to the Point! This is a waste of time, I got stuff to do!"

This reminds of me a great movie quote from *A Beautiful Mind*. The main character is a mathematical genius. At one point, he's forced to teach a class full of freshman to fulfill his requirements of research funding. The beginning of his first class, on the first day, he lets everyone know exactly how much he values his time by telling the eager young minds of tomorrow, *"This class will be a waste of your - and what is infinitely worse - my time."*

Leaders should not waste the precious time your team has given you. No one wants his or her time wasted. Time is a precious commodity that can never be given back. Harvey MacKay once said,

"Time is free, but it's priceless. You can't own it, but you can use it. You can't keep it, but you can spend it. Once you've lost it, you can never get it back."

Time is one of life's most precious gifts. When you think about blessing others just remember that you can make more money, but you can't make more time. Our lives are comprised of the time we have here on Earth, and the time we spend or INVEST, can never be returned.

As another wise person said,

"Time is precious… waste it wisely!"

Start on time and if you have the opportunity, let your team go early! Your team will appreciate all the work and forethought you've put into making this vision for worship happen. They will be more willing to give their time in future after seeing how you effectively crafted the rehearsal.

The Mark of a Powerful Rehearsal

- Start the Clock

1. Effectively Communicate the Start Time of rehearsal to everyone involved.
2. Make sure you start the rehearsal ON TIME!
3. Enforce the standards after they are set.
4. Make audible notice of people who are Late.
5. Keep track of the time.
6. Be Mindful of Everyone's Time.
7. Prepare a Rehearsal full of Substance
8. Don't Waste Time – Be Purposeful!

CHAPTER 8:

TALK TO YOUR TEAM

Welcome Your Team

The first thing your team should experience as they walk into your rehearsal is a warm and friendly welcome. This may seem like something small to pass over as you are reading, but as I've explained in previous chapters, every step plays a role in the framework of a Powerful Rehearsal.

The Environment

Have you ever been to the Disney Store? Back in the 90's, there seemed to be a location in every mall across the country and even in Japan. The number of these stores is nowhere near what it used to be. Through changes in ownership and a variety of other market trends, there are only 20 locations in the US today where you can walk into a retail environment and be completely encompassed by stuffed animals and toys from all your favorite Disney movies and shows.

When I was younger, I used to go the mall with my friends and play a game. The mission, should you choose to accept, was to see who could walk into the Disney Store undetected. Sounds simple, right? You had to traverse all the way to the back wall where there was a big screen playing movies behind the latest display of giant plush animals. You then had to return back towards the front and exit the store. You were allowed to take any path you like, circumventing displays and rounding islands of new toys. You could hide behind other customers in the store and even army crawl beside the front desk, which held the cash register. The only catch... you had to make the pass without any employee greeting you. This was a challenge. I don't recall ever succeeding, nor did I ever witness someone else succeeding. I don't think James Bond, Jason Bourne or Ethan Hunt could've completed this impossible mission. I came close a couple times. I'd enter the store, crouching beside a family of 4 or more who were walking in. I'd quickly scope out the rest of the store before hiding in a corner, counting a couple seconds, and making a dash to the back wall. I took a deep breath, my heart pounding in my chest, and moved along a different path for my exit. I was as sly as a fox, as I passed the Fox and Hound toys on my right. I stopped my gate just in time to avoid an employee speaking with a 6-year-old customer, took a hard left, another right and saw my goal straight in front of me. I quickened my pace, and with less than 10 feet from the sweet taste of victory I hear, "Welcome to Disney Store!"

"Gaaaahhhh, I almost had it!" I turned to face my opponent and said sheepishly, "...thank you..." I held my head in defeat as I stepped forward to my friends who were clapping and laughing. None of us had leveled up that day.

The Disney Store had a lot of things going for it. Whoever was the marketing genius behind building the "Disney Store Atmosphere," clearly communicated the expectations and standards for each employee. I can imagine the daily, weekly, and quarterly staff meetings with employers stressing the importance of welcoming customers to the store. After being welcomed like that with a smile, it was truly hard to not feel happy in a place with fun music and dancing / singing animals on screens around you.

I'm sure you can think of a couple other companies that have followed suit with creating an atmosphere unique or complementary to their brand. Go to a Chick-Fil-A, order anything off the menu and you're sure to hear the employee answer your request with a joyful, "My pleasure."

Michael Gerber, author of the best seller of The E-myth, encourages his clients to change their verbal approach to new customers. Try replacing,

"Can I help you?"

with,

"Hi, have you been here before?"

Those clients who switched have seen their sales increase by 16%. They're seeing this growth trend because by shifting the focus of their question just a small amount, they built an association with that person. This leads to a feeling of belonging and relationship as a returning customer who is known by the employee. The customer feels engaged, fully welcomed, and is more inclined to make a purchase in a place they are comfortable. If you don't remember a name, you can easily change your phrasing to, "Well, Hello! Its nice to see you again."

The Leader Sets the Tone

You are the leader and **You** set the tone for the atmosphere. Create an environment of warmth, inclusion, and thankfulness for each band member that walks through the doors. Remember that each person has sacrificed their time and other responsibilities to be there. This sacrifice alone should make you thankful they are in attendance. Think about the role you have planned for them on the team, how they fit into the vision for worship on the weekend, and you will understand how important they are to the success of the team. If you are missing one person, executing the vision for worship may not happen at all, or at least not the same. Without them you may have to change your plans, pick out a different song or scrap the ideas you've been preparing. So, each person taking part in the rehearsal warrants a warm welcome and gratitude for their participation!

Inclusion of All Team Members

We all have our own back-story, things in our childhood that made us who we are today. I'm sure many who read this book could echo my memories of not always being accepted by peers my age. Kids can be brutally honest. I was an overweight kid growing up. I was active and loved being adventurous, but also found comfort in food. I was picked on some, wasn't the most popular kid in class, and I didn't have the attention of the pretty girl I wanted to talk to. I had a fair share of sitting alone at lunch and feeling like I wasn't included like all the "cool kids" seemed to be.

I look back at those experiences now with a single thought… I wish the Me of today could go back and encourage the Me of back then. I don't have a DeLorean or any plutonium. I can't go back in time. So, instead I'll look at the positive. I learned a lot through those times alone. I was able to look at myself in those moments and see the same physical and emotional language telegraphed in others. I was given a gift that developed into a skill. It's almost like I could decode this secret language with my eyes. I could read the situation like Neo looking into the world of The Matrix.

There is message I see in the faces of others who are not "welcomed." They are all asking the same question: "I want to be part of a group. Please, will someone come sit by me?" Whether someone sitting alone will admit it or not, I've found more than 9 times out of 10, an action to address this desire will make their day. I still use this gift to read that desire today. Anytime I'm in an environment and see someone who is sitting alone and giving this message, I'll seek him or her out and work to engage them in conversation or include them in the activity.

What does this mean for you as a team leader? We are all human beings with the same intrinsic desires. We all want to be loved, included, to feel safe and loved. The atmosphere of a worship service begins the moment your team walks into the rehearsal. Each person on your team is a worship leader. A person in the church can be watching and led into God's presence by any musician, at any given moment. This is our responsibility, to lead others into the presence of God, and guess what…

The Presence of God is Welcoming to All!

John 3:16 - For God so loved the world (all of us!)…

Matthew 10:40 (NIV) 40 "Anyone who welcomes you welcomes me, and anyone who welcomes me welcomes the one who sent me.

Romans 15:7 (AMP) - 7 Therefore, [continue to] accept and welcome one another, just as Christ has accepted and welcomed us to the glory of [our great] God.

I have been both leader and servant at many different churches in my career. Every opportunity that I've had to lead a team, rehearsal, meeting, service or ministry, I have always sought to welcome and include others. I see inclusion as such a huge aspect of the Kingdom of God. Unfortunately, there are many churches that do not have "welcoming" and "inclusion" as values they seek to strengthen and uphold. Those churches are missing out on a key element to who God is and what it means to let God's will be done on Earth as it is in Heaven.

When your team walks through the door, make them feel they are walking into the very presence of God with a warm smile, and a joyful, "Hey, there you are!" Give them a hug, handshake, pat on the back, or whatever is appropriate. Make sure each person knows they are welcome every time they come to serve.

Connect through Story to Build Community

After welcoming the team at the start of the rehearsal, I often tell a little story about my week or something out of the ordinary that happened in my day. If I've got nothing I can recall, then I ask for someone else to share, especially if I already know they've done something pretty cool that would be neat for the team to hear. This is a great way to help everyone get to know each other a little better, build relationships and again allow people to be comfortable in the environment.

Did you ever participate in *Show and Tell* at school when you were young? It turns out, there was a lot more to it than meets the eye. I always thought it was just a special time for me to share what I'm passionate about. The whole class was looking at me. I was in charge. I had the power! I was young, I only saw the small immediate benefit of getting attention. What I didn't see then was the bigger picture, the benefit of becoming known more by my peers. I could have made a new friend by sharing a common interest and built relationships that would last a lifetime. By the way, I still have friends today who I've known since grade school.

Even if you're just sharing a small personal story, you

could be opening up the door to a new connection with someone else. Have fun with this process. It doesn't have to be anything too formal or complicated. Think about some conversation starters that'll give somewhere to go. I've used tons of different random ideas through the years. This makes me think of an old SNL sketch where comedian Mike Myers is hosting a TV show called *"Coffee Talk."* His over-the-top character poses the question, "Peanuts, ...neither a pea, nor a nut. Discuss!"

Talk through the Order

Give a brief overall picture of what the service will look like. Start with the beginning song and build your brief synopsis for each individual song and how one song will instrumentally and vocally lead into the other. You can make mention of different instrumental and vocal solos, and even talk about your transitions some, but overall you want to keep this time short. Making sure you've prepared your team, everyone should have their music either printed out, in books or 3 ring binders, or digitally on their tablets in front of them. Don't rehash talking through the order too much when they can just turn the page and see what comes next. If you go too fast for them, tell your team to follow along in their music and keep up! You want to go a little bit deeper into what happens before they turn that page, but you're not at the point of diving into the actual rehearsal portion yet.

You can share the different sort of atmosphere you want the band to create with each song. You want to illuminate a taste of that vision you have for the worship service. If they can see the vision, even a small part here, the rest of your rehearsal will flow much easier and you'll have an extra bit of energy throughout your time together. You'll notice the difference when you communicate your vision effectively; it's a really good feeling. You can open the floor to answer questions or take comments on different elements, but keep driving on to the next portion of rehearsal.

Talk through the Tough Spots

Now you want to continue the dialogue with your team as you go over some of the more challenging areas of the music. This time will serve to bring an overarching plan to the team members for what will be included in the rehearsal. You could start off with something like,

"Did everyone get a chance to dive into this new song? Man, the rhythm section is really complex in the chorus and continues to build with some crazy fast chord changes in the bridge. We're going to pay extra attention to the bass kick in these sections, otherwise we could get lost in all of the contrasting parts."

That's just an example, tailor fit your comments to each specific song. You want to lay out an idea to your team for how you will address these tough and challenging areas later on.

The Mark of a Powerful Rehearsal – Talk to Your Team

1. Welcome Your Team
2. The Environment
3. The Leader Sets the Tone
4. Inclusion of All Team Members
5. The Presence of God is Welcoming to All!
6. Connect through Story to Build Community
7. Talk through the Order
8. Talk through the Tough Spots

CHAPTER 9:

SOUND CHECK

The Importance of Sound Check

Leaders often overlook a solid sound check by trying to get going with the rehearsal. However, when done correctly a good sound check will setup your rehearsal and especially your service for a gigantic win. Every church deals with the "Sound" in either a positive or negative way. They are either positive the sound is good, or positive some people are going to have a negative experience. Haha! Sometimes you've just got to laugh at challenges and change your mindset! As Albert Einstein once said,

"We cannot solve our problems with the same thinking we used when we created them."

Let's change our thinking as we come to lead worship. Really focus one what is going to have a lasting effect on your musicians, the rehearsal, the service, and your church as you continue building Powerful Services.

The quality of sound produced by the musicians is critical in creating a truly worshipful environment. I'm not talking about perfection here or instructing you to buy an entirely new sound system. But, I believe you would agree that if any instrument is out of balance with another, it could become a point of distraction that would cause more attention than welcoming others into an atmosphere of worship. If the volume is too loud of the band collectively, it can be just as offensive or distracting as an individual instrument or vocal part out of place. The same can be said for band elements that are set too low in the mix. The key word in creating a beneficial sound check is to look for "Balance." An overall balance you want to create should be able to encompass the room in sound while not having a distracting element or part that sounds out of place. Each instrument and voice needs to work in accord with one another.

There are many varieties of Styles in worship music and that's a great! Gospel music can often accentuate Piano / Organ / Keys and Bass while Contemporary Christian music has recently featured Synthesizers with indiscriminant Pads and electronic programmed midi instruments. This will probably change in years to come as styles are always evolving.

Every style of worship music has a couple things in common and those are a significant Lead Vocal and a Prominent Instrument (typically ELG, ACG or Piano driven). Outside of these two ingredients in your style and the occasional solo, the rest of the band should be mixed in your sound to provide a mainly supportive role.

Here is the process for conducting an extensive and Solid Sound Check in rehearsal that will meet your stylistic needs and provide for a balanced overall sound.

Instruct New Members how to perform a Sound Check

Everyone's got to start sometime, right? I always make sure to go through the instructions for a sound check any time I have a new person joining the team and I often repeat the steps when they are still new for the first 2-3 rehearsals to make sure they've got the idea and the steps are ingrained. Use every occasion you go over the steps for a new person on the team as a teaching opportunity for the rest of the band. This will continue to build your routines and worship culture. If you have a new member joining your team every 4-6 months, you could be repeating your steps for a solid sound check a few times every quarter, which is not a bad thing! Your continual communication on this subject and others all serve to reinforce your standards.

How to Conduct a Solid Sound Check

In this section, I'll list out how to perform a Solid Sound Check with detailed steps. I'll also give you some pointers and extra suggestions in *Italics*.

1) The Process for FOH - Front Of House

a) As each individual is playing / singing, you want to make sure they are setup correctly first on the FOH board BEFORE you get to the monitors.

The FOH board will typically be the beginning of settings for each channel and is a foundation for the monitors. Depending on how your system is setup, if you change a gain setting on the FOH board it could change a level on your monitors. This is a very important time to make a quality setting for Input Gain on the FOH board, and then don't adjust it through the rehearsal or live service without communicating the change to the Worship Leader and Band Members.

I've had experiences where the FOH settings were changed during a live service, essentially cutting out the signal to my monitors. This created a big problem! Suddenly I was led to believe my battery died, the cord from my guitar was unplugged, or the power went out. This ultimately disconnected me from being fully engaged in worship and leading others to do the same. Changing FOH board settings during a service is one of my pet peeves and is very challenging to remain focused, especially after any changes should've been made in the Sound Check. Make sure you fully communicate this scenario with all of your sound techs and reinforce the importance of their correct settings in a Solid Sound Check.

b) During the Sound Check, your FOH sound tech is testing for several things:

i) Input Gain

(1) Make sure your Gain is set to allow a healthy signal. If you have a meter bridge or digital signal, you generally want to look for lights or LED's going from Green to consistently hanging around the Yellow, but not peaking into the Red lights. The sound tech may need to ask for more signal from an instrumentalist, or for a vocalist to sing louder.

ii) EQ

(1) Every channel needs to be EQ'd properly. This is an art form and science all its own. Simply, each instrument should sound in its amplified form the same way it does in its acoustic form without plugging into the sound system. You can then reinforce desired frequencies from there.

(2) A Flute will have a much different EQ than a Bass Guitar. In the same way, a Tenor Vocalist should be setup differently than a Soprano Vocalist.

iii) Output

(1) Mixing Level Faders need to be set with an idea of where the channel will be placed during the service.

(2) Your sound tech needs to have a bit of imagination and vision for how each channel will be mixed during the live service.

This step is a bit of a guessing game for your sound tech. Levels can and will change during a live service, but anticipating what you want your outcome to be in the future will better prepare you and help relieve stress in the live performance. You sound tech should have listened to the songs as well, knowing the mix / instrument solo requirements and what to look for as the rehearsal and service progresses.

2) Sound Check Each Individual Channel for FOH

a) Pick out one of the songs from the set to be rehearsed later and direct them which section to play / sing.

Its easiest and most effective to have everyone play / sing the same song if possible. Otherwise, you'll have vocalists singing their favorite parts of 3-5 different songs and you may get different keys, poor technique as they play / sing / or chaos as they jump into whatever section they choose.

b) Instruct team members to Play / Sing at the level of Performance, same volume and intensity that will be done in a service.

i.e. Play loudest Guitar Patches / Loudest Drum Sections / Strong Vocal Sections

This can feel intimidating and a little awkward, especially for new team members. Make sure to have other team members go first to model the correct way to sound check for the new team member.

c) Follow an Order

I find it easiest to go around the team members like their arrangement on the stage. It gives everyone an idea of when they need to be ready and it gives a pretty clear visual of who is on the team and how each member fills up the space and carries out different functions. This also allows easy communication from the stage to the FOH sound tech, especially if there is a distance. The next instrument in the circle is on deck for playing next, etc...

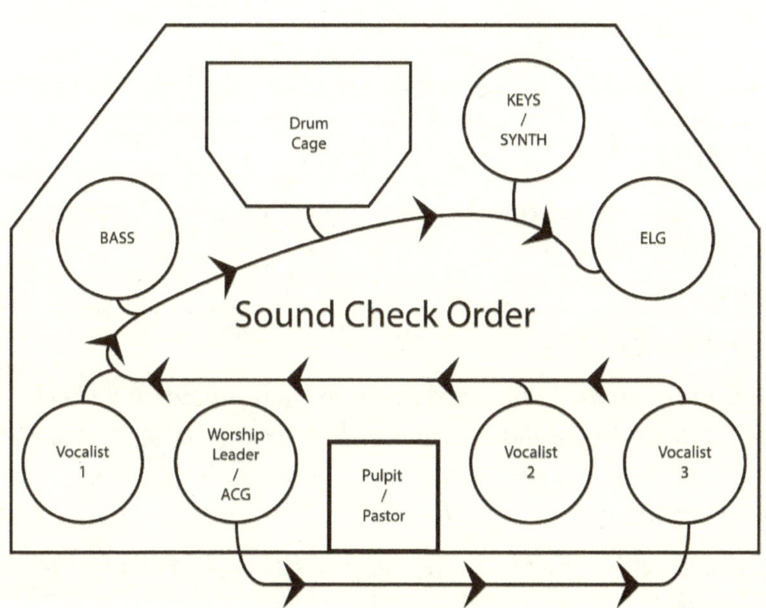

d) Start with Worship Leader's Instrument

I always start off sound check with my instrument first. I'll play a song selection we'll be rehearsing later, making sure the FOH sound tech has a comfortable level on my lead guitar / piano.

This kind of wakes up everyone to the idea of checking their instrument and gives them a model to follow.

I'm also now able to play the selection of the song I want the band to do their sound check on, and later on accompany the vocalists if needed and give them a cue for where to sing.

e) Move to Worship Leader's Voice

I then move onto my microphone, selecting part of a song to sing so the FOH sound tech can get a good level on my voice.

f) Check the rest of the Vocals

Have the vocalists sing a selection of the song you've chosen to go over later on in rehearsal. This is a foreshadowing to parts you'll be working on and a great warm up.

g) Go around the rest of the instruments, checking for their levels.

Ask between each instrument / voice if the FOH sound tech has a strong signal from the musician.

Communicate well and lead through each musician's check with a drive to the next person in line, being open for any questions or concerns and ready to help troubleshoot if problems arise.

Be prepared to relay information from your FOH sound tech to your band and vice versa. – You may need to tell the ELG player to turn down his amp, etc.

Remember to keep new team members in mind with where they will sound check in the order, and help them with encouragement if they are still unsure of what they need to do.

You may need to ask a team member to play again, play a different guitar patch, sing another section that fits their voice better or just sing / play louder if you don't think they are up to the level they should be in the live service.

Move quickly through each person's section. If you have your FOH and Monitors setup correctly, you should need no longer than 20-45 seconds for each person.

3) Monitors – In Ears / Wedges

a) Follow the previous Order for FOH Sound Check

b) Start with Worship Leader's Instrument

c) Move to Worship Leader's Voice

d) Check the rest of the Vocals

e) Go around the rest of the instruments, checking for their levels.

Ask between each instrument / voice if someone needs an adjustment in his or her monitors and if the FOH sound tech still has a strong signal from the musician.

4) Repeat steps if needed, but drive onto the next section of rehearsal

At this point you've welcomed everyone, created a warm and friendly environment, talked through the set list and shared a bit of your vision for the entire service. You've also gone through a Solid Sound Check. I try to aim for no more than 10-15 minutes to accomplish all of these steps. I have been in some situations where we spent more time on the sound check than actually rehearsing any music. Those exceptions typically involved troubleshooting equipment, tracing signal chains to make sure instruments were plugged into the right channel, and the inevitable changing of batteries in a failing pickup or microphone.

I believe "Congratulations" is in order! You're well on your way to building your Powerful Rehearsal.

The Mark of a Powerful Rehearsal

– Sound Check

1. The Importance of Sound Check
2. Instruct New Members how to perform a Sound Check
3. Steps to perform a Solid Sound Check

CHAPTER 10:

START FIRST SONG

You've made it this far, now it's time to really get into the music portion. There are a lot of components to Building a Powerful Rehearsal and many of those take place far before you go over any songs with your band. Everything you've prepared to this point will go on to make the rest of your time together more focused and effective.

Just as a side note in preparing the rehearsal for your team, I encourage you to always look for unique qualities important to every song you come across. This habit will keep your mind in tune to remember the same elements for use in rehearsals. For example; anytime I hear a new recording on the radio that I would like to cover in worship, I will listen to how the song is orchestrated. I pay close attention to the instruments that really need to be highlighted for that song and arrangement. As you're assembling a list of songs you want to incorporate into your worship team's play list, keep in mind the musical genre you're presenting for your band and congregation.

Ask yourself –

"Will our band be able to perform these new songs well? Is this new song going to fit in with the style of the service I'm trying to bring about and represent the vision God's given me?

Form in Songs

If you've ever studied Classical music, you are quite familiar with determining forms. Most of the music written hundreds of years ago followed popular formulas that are easy to identify. Some of these structures are; Theme and

Variations, Rondo Form, Sonata Form, and Sonata Rondo Form. The short explanation for these different structures is –

"the focus on one or more musical ideas and the repetition of those ideas in a particular order and arrangement."

These forms are most often notated as including an A, B, C, and sometimes D section. A three section Rondo form would be noted as A-B-A-C-A. In today's terms, you might find a song that would fit in that form and call the structure Chorus – Verse – Chorus – Bridge – Chorus. The music we have today is all built on the same identifiable structures... except for jazz, sometimes. Jazz musicians try to break the rules all the time.

If we didn't have rules and structures in music, we would be listening to an unending melody line that goes on forever, without familiarity, impossible to sing along with on first listen. Do you know the formula for Pi - **π**? (The mathematical one, not America's desert) It starts out with 3.14 and gets fuzzy for me after that. Mathematicians agree that we will never be able to calculate all the digits of pi because it is an irrational number, one that continues forever without any repeating pattern. Imagine singing a song that irrationally changes notes... for eternity. That sounds like a terrible reality.

Music has form so it can be understood and truly appreciated by the human mind. When you look at the form of each song you play, you'll see how the structure can change if you want to bring out certain elements or there are sections you wish to emphasize.

Because I talked about apple pie, now I'm thinking of the song American Pie by Don McLean. This song was written in 1971 and has roughly 6 verses and 6 choruses. The original recording is around eight and half minutes long. That's a pretty long song by most contemporary standards. If the artist did not make a difference between the Verse and the Chorus, it would not be the classic it is today. Instead, we have a singable melody and clear distinction between Verse and Chorus. When you see the structure, emphasize different sections, and your congregation knows when that powerful Chorus or Bridge is coming up, that will encourage you and others to sing out even more.

Most songs sections are pretty easy to identify. I won't go too deep here, but just so we're all on the same page, I use these signifiers.

- Intro
- Verse
- PreChorus
- Chorus
- Bridge
- Instrumental
- Vamp (repeat Chord progression)
- Outro / Ending

There are times in analyzing a new song where the author has placed in a ½ Bridge, or an Instrumental that has part of the lyrics from the Chorus in it. Don't stress out too much about what to call this part. No one is going to fight you over it. Just pick a section title that fits best and go with it. You can expand on the titles above easily by calling them – Chorus 2, Bridge 2, etc. I had a recent rehearsal where I was leading the team on a new song. We came to one part and I didn't agree with the section titles given in the lead chart from an online music distributor. So, I told the team, "Your chart says measure 42 is the start of the Chorus, but because its vastly different from the first Chorus, I'm going to call this section a Bridge." I feel I actually improved upon the chart and was able to lead my team better, taking out some possible confusion. It doesn't make sense to have two different sections titled the same.

The whole point of titling these sections is for you to be able to effectively communicate where you are in the music and pass on directions to your team.

Song Rehearsal Process

I have listed out my steps for what I call the Song Rehearsal Process, which you can follow to help develop each song in your rehearsal. Each one of these steps are vital to ensure you are leading your team with wisdom and depth. If followed correctly, you will see your team connecting with every segment needed to perform the song well.

Song Rehearsal Process
Step 1
– Song Evaluation –

Here is how I typically run through one of my songs in rehearsal. I create a Song Evaluation in my mind before going into rehearsal with the team. I suggest you write this evaluation down for each of your songs before you get the hang of it. Once you study this method and have used it multiple times, it will become like second nature any time you think about a song. Just as we talked about identifying different sections in Classical music, you are to distinguish the important sections of the songs you're playing. In studying the unique qualities of each small section, you'll better understand how these portions are a part of the whole. This will make you a greater musician as you focus on what really makes your songs come together. You will learn how to communicate this to other musicians.

Below, you will see how I have pretty much every section of the song listed and written down, with the addition of some variations in unique parts of the song. You can take this list and apply it to pretty much any song you're going to be working with, regardless of the tempo/ orchestration/ theme/ genre.

The point of this exercise is to get you to think about what is most important musically in this each song you do. From there, you will be able to work better with the team and help them understand the differences in each segment. Fill out this form, regarding each line as a question. List out any other ideas, answers, or other things that are notable and important to remember for each line of each song. I've added some notes of my own, just to give you an idea how you could do this quickly for each song. This is an important step in your growth as a musician and musical leader.

You will also find this evaluation list in the back of the book, in the resources section and online at www.Downpourintl.com

Song Evaluation Guide

A. Intro

a. Dynamics
b. Instrumentation and Musical Motifs

B. Verse 1

a. Dynamics
b. Instrumentation
c. Vocals – Melody / Lead Only Typically

C. PreChorus

a. Dynamics – Soft then Crescendo into Chorus
b. Instrumentation – Driving Rhythms
c. Vocals – Add BGV Lightly

D. Chorus

a. Dynamics – 1st time *mf*
b. Instrumentation – Pull back Instrumentation at start
c. Vocals – Strong, Add in Harmonies

E. Intro / Instrumental

a. Dynamics – Strong as in the beginning
b. Instrumentation – Same as in the beginning

F. Verse 2

a. Dynamics – Build up slightly from V1 level
b. Instrumentation – Add slightly more Overdrive in ELG, Stronger Bass
c. Vocals – Strong, Harmonies

G. PreChorus

a. Dynamics – Crescendo into Chorus
b. Instrumentation – Driving Rhythms
c. Vocals – Strong, Harmonies

H. Chorus

a. Dynamics – *f*
b. Instrumentation – Full Band, Everyone Driving
c. Vocals – Strong, Harmonies

I. Bridge

a. Repeats – Multiple, but no more than 3
b. Dynamics - Variations
c. Instrumentation – Highlight a different Instrument / Motif
d. Vocals – Strong, Harmonies

J. Chorus

a. Repeats – At Least 2
b. Dynamics - *ff*
c. Instrumentation – Full and Strong
d. Vocals – Strong, Harmonies

K. Intro / Outro / Instrumental

a. Dynamics – Same as in Beginning
b. Instrumentation - Same as in Beginning

Song Rehearsal Process
Step 2
- Talk Through the Song with Your Team -

In beginning the Music Rehearsal, just talk through the song first with your team. If your team has done this song before, then you don't have to say much but remind people of different areas of importance.

I can't tell you how many times I've played God of This City by Tomlin, or Mighty to Save by Hillsong. It's been a little while since I've used those songs in a worship service. If I were to use those songs this weekend, I may need a little refresher to hear some key elements in the recording I'd like to bring out. A fresh listen to the song may inspire me to create a new counter melody with a solo that'll bring a fresh take on an old favorite.

Now this next step is a tricky one, but I promise it has a lot of value and science behind it.

Song Rehearsal Process
Step 3
- 1st Run-Through -

Run through the song as far as you can, try to make it to the end WITHOUT STOPPING!

This is GOLD here! Using this little method will give you a lot of clues in how you need to focus your energy for each song and the rest of the rehearsal. This works especially when your team is reading it for the first time. You should be able to pick up on; how prepared your team is with the music given, who has and has not practiced solos, how well your weaker musicians are playing, and if your team understands and executes the correct dynamics needed for the song.

There may be a chance you have a team member who did not practice before rehearsal or didn't even listen to the music beforehand. You will soon discover who didn't do their homework by this first run-through. Unless your band mates are all paid, you can't fire that person. And if you want them to come back to church, I would recommend not firing them anyway just for missing a part.

During your first run-through, make note of any sectional "train wrecks" or trouble spots. You will need to deal with those later. Start building a written list, adding each trouble areas as you go along. You'll address those spots when you're breaking down the section fragments that need to be stronger. You can start doing this by making a mark in your music for each rough spot, circle a challenging rhythm, underline a passage or make a full written list on your page or a post-it note. As you get more comfortable in this practice, it will seem like second nature and you may not need to make a written list at all in the future.

Here are a few examples of a musical train wreck:

-The band gets to a section in a song and stops playing / singing while you (the leader) keep going.

-The Drummer drops out playing in a Bridge / Chorus or section that is different from the previous because there is a new drum beat - Cut Time / Meter Change

-There's a key change that no one is prepared for.

-There is a repeat, coda or first ending repeat leading to another portion of the song that some were not prepared for. The team just needs to look ahead in the music and know where the next section will lead. This is especially important if you are using lead charts instead of chord charts.

-You get to a portion in the song and it no longer sounds like the song you started with.

Don't worry or get upset when you have a train wreck in rehearsal. This is a much better time to have one than in a performance. It's going to happen, and every team goes through it. It's indicative of the learning process and it will probably happen again in another rehearsal as you present your team with more and more new music. Get it out now so you can work through those trouble areas and prevent them from appearing in that song again.

You will find as you present your team with more music, they will become more skilled with the ability of reading. You will see your number of train wrecks diminish. No one wants a train wreck. Your musicians will better prepare themselves, feel more comfortable in looking ahead, and they will take their own notes to prevent the catastrophic stopping of the music. They will want to produce a better product for the worship team. Everyone on the team should naturally develop a desire to become a more skilled musician.

God's word reveals he called gifted artisans by name to build the tabernacle in Exodus 31 (NKJV).

31 Then the Lord spoke to Moses, saying: 2 "See, I have called
by name Bezalel the son of Uri, the son of Hur, of the tribe of
Judah. 3 And I have filled him with the Spirit of God, in
wisdom, in understanding, in knowledge, and in all manner of
workmanship, 4 to design artistic works, to work in gold, in
silver, in bronze, 5 in cutting jewels for setting, in carving
wood, and to work in all manner of workmanship.

6 "And I, indeed I, have appointed with him Aholiab the son of

Ahisamach, of the tribe of Dan; and I have put wisdom in the hearts of all the gifted artisans, that they may make all that I have commanded you:

When we come together to serve the Lord, build His Church, and offer our gifts to Him in leading others in His presence to Worship, we need to be reminded of our heritage. God has called you and me by name for this great work and we are to give our Best!

Song Rehearsal Process
Step 4
– Status Check –

So, you've run through the song as far as you can and at this point you have survived your first playing of the song. Ask everyone if they need anything adjusted in their mix. This is a great time to do a Sound Check again with the FOH engineer and make any adjustments needed. With your team going through a song together for the first time, you and your team will now have a better idea of how your individual mix needs to be set for optimal performance and engagement. Your FOH engineer will also be able to do a more balanced Sound Check for your Mains after hearing the band go through a song together.

At this stage, remember to Be Kind to your sound engineer! This person is working hard to serve you and the whole team. Imagine you have asked the sound engineer to be the head chef for a dinner party and you've given them an hour to prepare. You want them to host your whole worship team today and a banquet for the whole church later on this week. Picture everyone sitting at the table, they bring out the food and something's wrong… The food tastes terrible! In all of the hustle to prepare, your chef / sound engineer forgot to season the food. They are not super confident with spices and just did they best they could. What do you do? Do you get up and help them add some salt and pepper to the different dishes? Do you cordially thank them for all their hard work and offer to assist in helping others enjoy their meal? Do you smash your plate on the floor and yell at the top of your lungs, "Come on! Can't you do anything right!?!?"

I hope you get the point. This is another important area to model the behavior of a servant leader.

Song Rehearsal Process
Step 5
– Run the Trouble Spot – Communicate –

After the First Song Run-through and Second Sound Check, talk about the train wrecks or trouble spots and how you're going to go over those again until they are correctly executed. Using your own skill set, you as the leader should Play or Sing through sections to illustrate how they should be.

This part always makes me smile as I see personality and individuality shine through with each leader I work with. I'm very comfortable singing through sections and using my mouth to sort of "beat box" my way through percussion rhythms. I will also illustrate rhythms by clapping them myself, then having everyone clap the rhythm together if its really challenging.

I had a Jazz Band conductor in college that was a Trombone Performance major. Anytime he would count off the song or give instruction to a rhythm section, his own method was saying in a percussive manner, "1, 2, 3, Chun, Chun, CHUN!" (Imagine conducting this in 6/8 time.) Where he got his "Chun, Chun, CHUN" method, I don't know. But, it worked for him. Find what works for you!

You don't have to personally model every part for each vocal line and instrument. I could feel a huge weight lifted off my shoulders when I learned this many years ago. Even if you are not the most skilled and proficient musician for every instrument represented on your team, find a way to communicate to each one of your respective instrumentalists and vocalists. You can do this by emulating their instrument in some way. If you're not a drummer but want to emulate how a drumbeat should go, you can try clapping your hands, tapping you're your legs, tapping on a music stand, or "beat boxing." Look for any method that will give your drummer an idea of the rhythm you want them to produce. Not a great guitar player? You can tell guitarists to listen to the recording several times, you could play their lead line on another instrument for them, or you could have another more advanced instrumentalist on your team show them on a similar instrument.

If you're looking to imitate something with a vocalist, this could be a little more challenging. Some vocalists have a hard time doing something vocally that is modeled from an instrument. One of the best exercises I learned when I was in school was to listen to other vocalists. Not a great Vocalist? You could have a set of recordings on hand with different vocalists producing the same song, possibly both male and female lead versions. Have examples ready of what you want your team members to sound like or replicate. Give them options and encourage them to grow in their skill.

Song Rehearsal Process
Step 6
- Unique Gifts -

I don't believe in creating an exact duplicate of any worship recording or band. The recordings give a great representation of what the artist or songwriter was looking to create, but I believe God is looking for individuality and expressiveness to rise out of every worshiper. Otherwise, we're just giving someone else's gift of worship as our own. Your unique gift mix, fully alive and operating at 100% of its potential, will always be greater than an attempt to copy someone else's.

I like how St. Irenaeus put it,

"The glory of God is man fully alive."

In this context, in regards to worship, imagine everyone you know giving their all to sing / play / shout and praise the Lord. Can you imagine that? What a wonderful worship service that would be. I believe God's presence would surely reside there in a Powerful way!

I remember my vocal coach in college had me go to the library and get several recordings of famous tenors like Fritz Wunderlich. I would spend hours in the music lab listening to this incredible tenor belting out insanely high, seemingly falsetto tones. He sang with such clarity and power. This was an assignment that left me speechless and a little frustrated. I would then go to the practice rooms, pull out my music and try to emulate the same sound and production value as he did.

I'm Ken Jansen, not Fritz Wunderlich. I have a voice that God gave me by His very own design. I am not meant to be a copy of anyone else. However, I can learn a lot from other skilled artists in how to use my voice. I have the capacity to learn how those artists worked so hard, developed more understanding, and became great craftsmen. I can then apply this knowledge to my own skillset. I am all for learning from the hard work of others.

When it comes time to shine though, we are meant to reveal our gift in the unique way God intended. Whether you're playing a solo, keeping that rhythm section steady, or singing the lead, I encourage you to make those parts yours! Worship in the way that you were uniquely designed to and you will encounter God's presence like never before.

Song Rehearsal Process
Step 7
– Highlight Specifics –

When you're working with your different team members individually, make sure in your communication to highlight the specific Rhythms (are they Straight / Syncopated / Contrasting), Melodic lines (which part has the melody / which parts are harmony), and Motifs that make the song unique.

Motifs are small musical ideas that can easily be recognized in a song. If you are familiar with minimalism as it applies to music, you will most likely be able to hear this from the music of Coldplay. Minimalism in music is not a new idea. As far as we can tell, the idea of repeating small musical phrases has been around since the early years when music was first written down. If you study Gregorian Chant, you'll find many repetitive sections harmonizing within different parts. You see this occurring in different genres and ages of music creation throughout history.

The thing I like to point out to new students about the band Coldplay is that it's very easy to pick out. The lead singer and instrumentalist of this band is a piano player. If you listen to the song *Clocks*, you obviously hear a higher octave, small section of piano notes that are repeated with a light variation to the pitch. This small musical idea is repeated not only in the intro, but various interludes and other sections of the song. You hear it coming back often. It's a recognizable theme that appears here and there throughout the song.

Worship music can contain this composition tool as well. You often hear artists write different motifs in a song to be a recognizable return of an Intro, Chorus, or Bridge. Hillsong produced a worship album called *Mighty to Save* in 2006. It's gone on to sell millions of copies worldwide, introducing popular songs like the album title *Mighty to Save, From the Inside Out*, and *Take it All.* You can certainly hear the aspect of minimal in the song *Take it All.* There's an electric guitar part in the Intro that is very easy to identify. To me it sticks out like a sore thumb, I can't NOT hear it. This motif is like one of those optical illusions your brain finally sees, and then you have a hard time seeing the image as you did before. I cannot imagine this song without this motif, it just wouldn't be the same without that small group of notes from the ELG. Anytime that song starts, you know where the rest of it is going and your brain fills in the dots.

Don't shy away from musical motifs like this, they can be a lot of fun to work with and empowering to musicians on your team. If they are the instrumentalist with the musical motif to play and get everyone excited about the upcoming song, it's like they are introducing the song to the congregation and the rest of the band is backing them up. It's a lot of fun when people get excited about a musical motif and they know that this is a particular praise song, or a worship song with a specific theme. A few familiar notes can help foreshadow something very powerful in the next section of the worship service. People can have emotional attachments to small musical phrases. They're very easy to remember.

Bittersweet Symphony by The Verve gives me goodtime feels every time I hear it. The repetitive string motif reminds of a summer when I was younger, driving down the road with the window down on a beautiful sunny day. I like that song. On the other hand, I have a pretty negative reaction to the 90's pop song *Tom's Diner* by Suzanne Vega. I haven't heard that song for years, but when I think about the first little motif, I can't get it out of my head for the rest of the day. For the sake of your own sanity, I warn you. Look that one up at your own risk.

Song Rehearsal Process
Step 8
– Move On –

Another key point in this part of the rehearsal is to Move On! Don't feel like you have to run the song more than 3-4 times. This is of course assuming you have run through several parts of the song, or the song as a whole, with some amount of success. You've addressed what is important about the song and also given valuable rehearsal practices in musical instruction at this point. Make sure you do not overwork this one particular song. Remember, there are many other things to do in this rehearsal and we have just begun the music portion. Don't waste all your time for rehearsal on the first song. Be mindful of driving forward and remember your syllabus. Remember how much more you have to accomplish for the rest of the rehearsal time.

The Mark of a Powerful Rehearsal

– Start First Song

1. Talk Through the Song with Your Team
2. Form in Songs
3. Song Rehearsal Process
    1. Song Evaluation
    2. Talk Through the Song with Your Team
    3. 1st Run-Through
    4. Status Check
    5. Run the Trouble Spot – Communicate
    6. Unique Gifts
    7. Highlight Specifics
    8. Move On

CHAPTER 11:

START NEXT SONG

You're on a roll now, time to start the next song. This may seem like an oversimplified step, but after the momentum you created and progress accomplished in the first song, you want to keep it up. The drive you create going from the first song to the next will establish the pace for the rest of your rehearsal. You will often have a sweet taste of victory when the band has succeeded rehearsing the first song well. You may feel the draw to keep working on that first song and stay there in the atmosphere of achievement, but you need to keep working! Push on to the unknown challenges of the next songs. Keep progressing so that every song in your set list has been completed with the same focus and dedication.

Patterns in Musical Technique

Remind your team of any areas that were a challenge in the previous song so they may apply the same instruction to this next song. If you know that certain members of your team are having a problem with a particular rhythm, or vocalists are striving to harmonize in a certain way, then remind them of the same tactics used in similar sections of the previous song. You are building Patterns in Musical Technique for your team members to learn and use throughout the rehearsal. For example, you may ask a Tenor vocalist to sing a low harmony on one song. You will most likely have the same arrangement of vocalists on your team for the entire set. So, helping the Tenor find the area where he is to sing (high or low), will help him quickly find the same harmony on other songs. This makes his part easier once he understands his part in relation to others. This also relieves you from teaching him how to find his harmony on every song, thus saving you time and effort. Be prepared to identify areas where the harmonies are not together and go over those in more depth.

Use this tactic with other instruments as well. I often tell my ACG players to focus on a driving rhythm through several songs, unless there is a point where I want to highlight another instrument or want the ACG to lightly arpeggiate some chords. This player is then thinking throughout most of the rehearsal, "I need to find a driving rhythm on this song. I can do this without the consultation of the Leader. I'll keep playing in this way until told otherwise." If you've ever heard of Ron Popeil, the Infomercial King, he used to have a catch phrase he'd say when giving a demo of his brand-new kitchen rotisserie. "Set It and Forget It!"

Set your musicians in motion and allow them to bring their own parts to life. Allow them to come alive and express their own unique ability to worship. Free yourself from micromanaging your team. You do not have to carry the weight of directing every single note for each musician. That's too much stress to bear and you don't have enough time to do that in a 2-hour rehearsal.

Your responsibility as a Leader is to reign in all the different parts, give instruction on technique, and form a unified sound. Remember that Barrel of Monkeys? You want to connect all those parts together, but you do not have tell each person how to be a Monkey; God has already designed them with gifts and abilities. You get the opportunity to help their skills grow and assemble these gifts into an offering of Worship.

Confidence

Instill Confidence in your team members. Throughout the entire rehearsal you are enhancing their own abilities of how to play and sing each song. Every song will have its own unique qualities and necessities, both instrumentally and vocally. You will have some fast songs relying on driving rhythms and intensely high vocal melodies. Other songs will need focus on keeping a steady slow tempo with soft vocal harmonies. As you go through each song and you draw on examples of past sections (including similar rhythms or melodies), you will be able to give illustrations of how to perform in this next piece.

Now that you're on the second song, you basically want to recycle all the same steps that you used in introducing and rehearsing the first song. I advise you to go back to Chapter 11 and make sure you are completely confident in each one of the steps listed out there. Study it! Memorize it!

Here's a little assignment for you –

1. Get out a piece of paper and a pen / or pencil. (You have to do this by hand, it cannot be on a computer. This assignment will instill these rehearsal steps into your brain using a tactile-kinesthetic learning technique)
2. Write down the 8 steps of the Song Rehearsal Process – 20 times.
3. Write down the Song Evaluation titles A-K including each sub-heading – 20 times.
4. If you cannot repeat the steps word for word, or write them down without looking in the book, do the assignment again.

Remember, you can also flip to the end of this book where you will find a chart listed in the appendix. Go online to DownpourIntl.com and download resources that go along with this book.

A quick reminder for the Song Rehearsal Process, talk through the song with your team. Point out important sections and work them for a brief amount of time. Make sure you take notice of any train wrecks or trouble spots.

Continue this Song Rehearsal Process for as many songs as you have in your set.

The Mark of a Powerful Rehearsal

- Start Next Song

1. Patterns in Musical Technique
2. Confidence

CHAPTER 12:

GO THROUGH YOUR SET BACKWARDS

This sounds like a crazy almost counter intuitive method for rehearsals, but I promise it works. I'm not suggesting you literally play a song backwards. Start from the song that you just went over, then go over the previous song, working back through your set towards the first song.

Lessons from Papaw

My grandfather, Kenneth Crocker (affectionately known as Papaw), was one of the hardest working men I've ever known. He was brilliant. He had incredible passion for God and a love for music, beauty, art and engineering. He pastored and built several churches from the 50's all the way through the 80's. Back then he did a lot of manual work by his very own hands. I have a picture of him sitting on top of a ladder affixed to the top of a crane. Over 30 feet in the air, he steadied and bolted together two massive wooden beams that were the main structure of the church roof. No one else on the construction crew would do it. He was fearless. He always focused on doing what had to be done. If there was anyone who could figure out a way to do it, it was him.

Papaw had a computer when I was young, but software in those days was nowhere near as user friendly as it is today. I remember sitting with him as he'd be working to write an article, attempting to understand the complicated and otherworldly tool known as Microsoft Word. I'd always hear him say, "There's got to be a better way to do this." He was always looking for an easier way to accomplish a task, a more efficient process that would save time and effort. He would often spend hours learning how to use a simple function in MS Word that would save him a small amount of time in the future. That small amount of time would add up more and more every time he would use that function, thus making his efforts worthwhile.

I learned so much from Papaw. I find myself doing the same things he did. I will spend hours researching, learning, and experimenting with different methods to perfect an easier way to accomplish a task. Sometimes my efforts don't produce the outcome I'm looking for. At other times, I have a massive breakthrough and feel like the smartest person in the world. The main objective I have is to develop a better way of doing things. Through my persistence, I am able to increase my efficiency and potential amount of production. This is a process of training my mind to establish the best practices for any task before me, whether that be rehearsing a song or efficiently mowing the grass with a particular pattern in the yard.

Ducktales was one of my favorite cartoons when I was a kid. I used to love the adventures, problem solving, and what I thought of as valuable life lessons inherent in each episode. While I learned an untold amount of life skills from Papaw, I also picked up a few gems from Scrooge McDuck. One quote from a particular show has always stuck in my mind as being completely brilliant. I've always thought of it any time I've faced a new challenge and can honestly see Papaw saying the same thing, that's probably why I love it so much. The quote comes from a scene where Scrooge is telling his young nephews about one of his earliest jobs. He's shining shoes to save money to come to America. He wanted to build his savings as quickly as possible and understood that the amount of shoe shines he was able to complete quickly was in direct correlation to his growth in profit.

Higher Production Amount = Greater Profits.

Scrooge took his father's advice, **"Work Smarter, Not Harder."** He used his father's suspenders and a bicycle to create a contraption providing service to 4 customers at once. This small illustration has influenced me for the rest of my life. It's inspired me to raise more questions. What can we do if we think outside the box? Is there a way we could become more productive? We might look strange in trying new methods, but is it possible we could create something greater than we could've imagined before?

I want to Work Smarter, Not Harder.

This method of going backwards through your set is something I've personally used for years and I find it's the most effective way of helping your team develop a full understanding the service order. You could say this is my "suspender – bike contraption." It's strange, sounds out of place and like it wouldn't work, but it's a method that uses the mechanics of the mind to build connections in rehearsal. I've seen it work over and over again and I know it'll prove beneficial to you and your team.

Hacking the Mind in Rehearsal

You'll often hear the word "Hack" in common speech today and it doesn't have such a negative connotation as it used to. Search the web for "useful kitchen hacks" and you'll be using a melon baller to MacGyver your way through life before you know it!

I want to be excellent at everything I do. Sometimes that desire is a real burden. I have even developed tunnel vision to become a better multitasker. Yeah... it's serious! As funny as that seems, I've always had a desire to find of a better way of doing things. I'm highly interested in different ways of "Hacking the human brain," and following steps to help myself produce at a higher level. I am not an advocate for taking drugs or medicating for things your body was designed to do naturally. However, there was a movie that came out years ago called *Limitless*. Scientists theorize that we humans only use about 10% of brain power. The premise of this film was that there was a drug developed to help access 100% of the mind's potential. Imagine what you could accomplish if you were 90% smarter? There was another movie produced a few years after this one later called *Lucy*, same kind of idea.

I view the human mind as an amazing "machine." Our brains are constantly functioning, completing our thoughts and continuing to work on problems in our subconscious. Have you ever had a weird dream that wakes up you, and you think about how that dream correlated to stressful challenges you faced during the day? Maybe you are struggling with something going on in your life right now. When you sleep at night, the subconscious portion of your brain is producing different ways to overcome those challenges. Your mind wants to resolve the problem. It keeps working whether you realize it or not. Do you typically have to think about every single breath you take, breathing in… breathing out? Do you have to remember to blink your eyes when they get dry? No, there are some things your mind takes care of automatically. It's incredible how our mind functions and continues to develop solutions without our conscious ability to recognize its activity.

There is a point to going backwards through your set, rehearsing a song and moving on without finalizing exactly how those trouble spots are going to get worked out. The point is to let our brains have a little space and freedom to work. In doing so, we give the subconscious a little bit of elbow room to work out different musical techniques and needs in performance without us over exhausting our mental resources.

I must confess, I am not the world's greatest multitasker. I've had many discussions with my wife about how I can easily develop tunnel vision. When my mind is set on completing something on my to do list, I want to use all the resources I have to focus on that project. I have always been uncomfortable taking personality tests that ask questions like, "Do you get frustrated when somebody interrupts your work?" Of course, I do! I know exactly what the test is trying to determine.

1. How well does Ken work in certain situations?
2. How can the employer best communicate with Ken?
3. Does Ken fit well in this job or position?

With a greater understanding of how the human brain works, we can help our teams to learn a song quicker and with a more profound comprehension. They will become more confident in the learning process as it is structured in a rehearsal setting. Remember, Worship Leaders are also teachers. We are developing educational methods for working with each of our team members, just like your favorite teacher or professor in school. Some of your band may not understand the purpose of going backwards through the set. Just encourage them. You can tell them that this is a method that helps every mind access its full potential.

Going backwards through the set helps to give another perspective of the progression of the service. As I've said before, one of the most important aspects of rehearsal is communicating with your team. You are helping them understand the movement of one song to the next, the progression of worship themes, and also their part to play in this service. At this point in rehearsal, you have progressed through each song as it will be done in the performance. Going through the songs in reverse will help everyone to see how the dynamics, tempo, and the theme relates to each song. They will better understand the direction you are looking to take everyone in the live worship set.

Let's say that you have a meeting 10 miles from your house. Unless you live in an area surrounded by large farms, there's no doubt you will be taking a few turns. Imagine with me you're going down this long road, looking to get to your meeting destination and have to drive over a few hills, through a couple valleys, cross a couple bridges, and finally arriving at your destination. The first time you travel this road, you may not know exactly where you're going. You can have an idea, but it's largely unfamiliar. After your meeting, as you return back home, you start to recognize different landmarks and parts of the road you saw before. You better understand the route that you have taken.

I took a vacation with my family to Florida this year. We currently live in Missouri and I drove the whole way.

We traveled through the countryside of South East Missouri - turned South to go through Memphis, TN - headed down Interstate 22 to go through Birmingham, AL - which led to Interstate 65 through Montgomery, AL - and on south to our destination in Florida. It was a long trip with several passes through small towns. Even though I confidently followed the GPS directions on my phone, I still felt unsure. I imagined a guy in the back of my head, sitting at a table, with a soft voice who kept saying, "I have no idea where I'm at." I was in Middle Earth! Like Gandalf leading the fellowship through the Mines of Moria. At the fork in the road he admits, "I have no memory of this place."

The journey from Missouri to Florida seemed to last forever. After our vacation, as I was driving us back home, I saw landmarks I remembered from the trip down. I recognized where I was. I was able to gauge the travel time in accordance with my location. Our return trip seemed remarkably shorter. I experience this all the time on long road trips. How about you? Our minds seem to experience time differently as we encounter the familiar.

This is something that our brain processes every day as we get a more complete picture of the world around us. There are a lot of things that go unnoticed as we travel down each road in life. When we turn around and take the same road back, locations we did not notice before may appear as something worth attention now. I don't know how many times I've driven down the same road and suddenly noticed a house with a certain color paint job, or there's a funny looking mailbox I had never seen before.

Focus on the Challenging Sections

Remember all those sections that were troublesome the first time you went through the songs? As you've gone through each song, you need to keep a record of all those trouble spots either written down or in your mind. You want to see these sections come together and become fluid with the rest of the songs. I encourage you to take some notes during rehearsal, either on a notepad, your music, or a digital device. You could do something as simple as circling a portion of a lead sheet or chord chart. Whatever your method is, you need to remember where those trouble sections are to address them fully. As you get more comfortable with the Song Rehearsal Process, you'll be able to recall more on-the-fly and remember which challenging section belongs to what song in the set.

Now you can spend some more time with each challenging section as you go back through your song set. Rework some of the portions you have done before. You can even try some different techniques in musical execution. It's interesting to see at this point how your musicians remember the trouble spot and face the challenges that they encountered before. Notice how much more confidence they have going over the section now. I'm always amazed how a little time away from a specific train wreck section will allow a musician to figure it out in his mind. Even as we're rehearsing different songs and learning new information, they're able to come back to a previous challenge and say, "Alright, I remember this part and now we're going to get it!" Remember, their minds are constantly working to resolve the challenge of performing correctly.

Trouble spots can be the most fun! Challenging sections, when done right, really make the band shine and the song come alive. You may have a section in a song you have worked on over and over again, to make it sound just like the recording. Say there is a particular syncopated rhythm or start / stop that you just could not get everyone on before, and now the band has got it... that's a great feeling! You will see this excitement and energy arise, especially with new musicians who have joined the team. Their confidence has grown throughout the rehearsal. Going back through the songs now with everyone feeling surer about the placement of the songs, the dynamics, the motifs and intricate musical demands, your band will sound more full and excited to perform using all of the rehearsal techniques they have learned.

Encouragement

Encourage your band at this point! They have already achieved so much by going through each one of the songs, and now going through all of the songs again in reverse order. You can make note of challenging portions that still need some work. But, here's a great place to tell the band how well they've done and how excited you are with what they've accomplished so far. Remember how we are building confidence in our teams. We want to give them positive reinforcement that is authentic and not just fluff.

I've had many professors in school and other team leaders I've worked with who rarely, if ever, gave out a positive comment. Some may think this stretches your team to earn the slightest word of praise. I prefer to create an environment where everyone feels welcomed and encouraged in a positive way to use his or her gifts.

I'm reminded of the film *The Money Pit.* There's a scene with Max, the strict symphony orchestra conductor who has incredibly high standards. His orchestra has just finished recording part of an opera. In contrast to his typically prevalent verbal abuse, you hear him give a few rare uplifting words about his team.

> *"That was... not so bad (with a small smirk on his face)."*
>
> *The recording engineer shouts from the back of the auditorium, "Are you happy with that one?"*
>
> *Max answers, "I am not unhappy with it. It's the best that miserable symphony has ever sounded.*

(turning to the orchestra) You have my congratulations and you may go home."

When can I audition to be part of that group (sarcastically)? Oh, never mind, I'd rather not.

You may have a team member who is used to receiving a lot of negative comments in their life. Your positive encouragement in a worship atmosphere may be one of the few occasions that draw them into God's spirit. Have you ever had someone criticize you at work in front of others? Have you been critiqued in an activity where there were other people standing around listening, watching, seeing how you will respond? This can happen in sports all the time, church staff meetings, and even on a worship team. It can be pretty intimidating.

Creating an environment of positive energy is just part of what the Holy Spirit does within us. **God's light within us should affect the world around us**. You still need to address if someone plays a wrong note, but do so in a loving manner. Being uplifting to your team member is not a weakness. It will not remove the drive for them to give their best as an offering in worship. This creates an environment that encourages them to give their heart, as well as the correct performance technique.

I hope you understand a worship leader should always seek to give the absolute best. I am extremely passionate about this area of ministry and leading others. I fully believe you can engage more people in worship and create a more inviting atmosphere for God's presence by using positive reinforcement with your team. This philosophy of leadership will always be more Powerful than demanding excellence of musical performance in a manner that cuts someone down, or strips away their confidence.

Proverbs 16:24 (AMP) "Pleasant words are like a honeycomb, Sweet and delightful to the soul and healing to the body."

The Mark of a Powerful Rehearsal

– Go Through Your Set Backwards

1. Hacking the Mind in Rehearsal
2. Focus on the Challenging Sections
3. Encouragement

CHAPTER 13:

TAKE STOCK OF THE WHOLE SET

At this point in the rehearsal you should be feeling pretty comfortable with how things are coming together. Now take stock of the whole set, evaluating how you've achieved your goals. Remember the vision you first started out with in planning this service. Let's look at what has been accomplished so far.

1. You have communicated the vision for the service to your team.
2. You've gone through each song multiple times.
3. Special attention and instruction has been given to help your musicians better perform the challenging sections.
4. You have increased everyone's confidence in performing each song.

Creative Flexibility

Compile a checklist of all you've accomplished as you continue to drive through the end of rehearsal. This will help you determine if the work you've completed is building your original vision for the service. This list is just for you. Don't communicate this part to the rest of your team, but you can be honest with yourself. You have a responsibility to create a complete rehearsal that prepares your team for what God wants to bring about in your church. If a piece just isn't coming together, regardless of how much effort has gone into "making it work," then let it go. Embrace the freedom to change things up.

God can work through any vehicle He chooses. It's important to recognize the essentials for God to move in a service do not rely on a perfected instrumental solo, or performing an exact replica of a recording by the original artist. When we give our offering of worship, God takes it and uses it as He wishes. Allow the pressure to fall off your shoulders. Open your eyes and be willing to using different methods to create an environment of worship.

I bet there is another song that conveys the same theme as the one you're trying to use. Would a different song be easier to play for your team? If your instrumentalists are struggling, is there another musician on your team who could play the solo on a different instrument (i.e. ELG solo turns into a Piano solo)? This would be a great opportunity to use a recorded part in a Click Track if you have no other option. You may have a lighting cue that seemed great in concept but is really distracting when you finally see it in person. Let's change that lighting element to something different and see how it works. Sometimes you really have to encourage yourself as the leader. Allow yourself to think outside the box and be flexible in accepting other alternatives that will bring about the same vision in a slightly different way.

Remember Jesus - Our Creator

Jesus is the ultimate Creator. Scripture says in, Colossians 1:15-20 (NIV),

"15 The Son is the image of the invisible God, the firstborn
over all creation. 16 For in him all things were created: things in
heaven and on earth, visible and invisible, whether thrones or
powers or rulers or authorities; all things have been created
through him and for him. 17 He is before all things, and in him
all things hold together. 18 And he is the head of the body, the
church; he is the beginning and the firstborn from among the
dead, so that in everything he might have the supremacy. 19 For
God was pleased to have all his fullness dwell in him, 20 and

through him to reconcile to himself all things, whether things on earth or things in heaven, by making peace through his blood, shed on the cross."

If we truly have a personal relationship with Jesus, then we should be the most creative people on the planet! My thoughts dwell on this often, "I want my art and creativity to be reflective of a living and loving creator, able to express majesty and beauty, worthy of the Son of God." I want my Heavenly Father to be proud of me. I am driven by this thought.

However, I often speak words to myself that are not life-giving. I feel the draw to be saved by works, but I know that is not what God's all about. The free gift of Grace is something I just can't comprehend. It's beyond me and incredible. I don't understand it. But, my world changes when I receive this Grace, which is given continually. I see how much love God is just waiting to pour out on us. His blessings are unending. He loves every gift I have to offer, no matter how small it measures or how I try to say its not good enough. He is proud of me! His word says in Zephaniah 3:17 (AMP),

"The LORD your God is in your midst, A Warrior who saves. ***He will rejoice over you with joy;*** *He will be quiet in His love [making no mention of your past sins],* ***He will rejoice over you with shouts of joy****."*

The word "rejoice" in these verses can also be translated as "dancing." So, God's word says that He is so proud of us; He's literally shouting and dancing over us! Let that sink in for a few minutes.... How different is your mindset now as you face a seemingly impossible challenge?

I declare this over you right now: You have a loving God who will not let you fail, for through Him all things are possible. He is excited about every aspect of you, so much that He's filling Heaven with shouts of joy... for You! Carry this truth with you throughout today, tomorrow and the next days. We have been called to fulfill a great position, and we are not in this alone.

Ask the Right Questions

In wrapping up this evaluation of where your rehearsal is, determining your current status of "making progress" or "still needing some work," ask yourself some important questions.

1. Are there any other areas you need to go over again?

2. How has your team come along in the rehearsal?

3. Is there one team member that is struggling more than the others?

4. Do you need to find another team member to help out for this weekend?

5. Do you need to replace any of the songs or switch out a song for another one the team knows better?

6. Are these songs fulfilling the vision you originally had for this service?

Depending on what your answers are to the questions above, the last portion of your rehearsal could be left up to some light communication or some further rehearsal with individuals who need some more music instruction. Whatever the case is, don't worry! I've had many rehearsals where I've asked all of these questions and felt like I needed a drastic change to better prepare for the service.

In some churches, you may find that the pressure to perform is greater than the acceptance of a positive environment. It's really unfortunate but a reality for many worship leaders and pastors. I served at a church where the leadership spent more time arguing about the performance quality of the musicians rather than acknowledging how people were engaging in worship and the spiritual development of the people on the team and in the congregation. They really missed the whole point of worship at that church, it was very sad. I did my best with the teams and created Powerful Rehearsals. We had awesome worship services and I just had to pray the hearts of those "leaders" would be changed.

Back to the checklist, take each question one at a time. Resolve what you can and seek to do the absolute best anyone could in your position. You may need to readjust your vision to make sure it fits with your team's capabilities and resources. If you can't pull off a brand-new worship song well, don't do it. If you don't have a capable ELG soloist to handle the parts in *Christmas Eve in Sarajevo* by TSO, maybe you shouldn't do it.

I by no means am saying you should lessen the greatness of what God has called you to do in this service. However, you need to be realistic in putting together a set that will help your team look good as well as fulfill the vision God has called you to bring about. The most important thing you can do is - Give Your Best. That gift you offer, in a Holy sacrifice, will bring glory to God. When it's authentic, filled with joy and passion, your gift of worship invites others into an atmosphere of worship. You create a place for others to connect with God. He then blesses your efforts according to His will. You may need to make several changes. You may have to adjust your personal expectations according to what can be done in your church and with your team, but that's the job description of a worship leader.

Do Your Best, Give God the Rest.

The Mark of a Powerful Rehearsal

- Take Stock of the Whole Set

1. Creative Flexibility
2. Jesus Our Creator
3. Ask the Right Questions

CHAPTER 14:

TRANSITIONS

Transitions are the glue that holds everything together in your worship set. There is nothing that will hinder the momentum of a great time in worship like a bad transition from one song to another. These moments are highly important and should not be overlooked.

If you are a fan of science and physics like me, then you are familiar with the term "Inertia."

Let's define this in a couple ways –

Inertia – the tendency of an object to stay at rest or in motion

- **Newton's First Law of Motion** - the property of matter by which it retains its state of rest or its velocity along a straight line so long as it is not acted upon by an external force.
- **In regards to Worship** – the energy in a worship set will continue in its state of motion until acted on by an outside force.

I believe Inertia applies to worship sets very well. If you think about each song having its own energy, driving forward to the next song, then the worship set will keep driving in that direction unless something stops it. There could be many things that create a metaphorical speed bump in your progression. I've experienced several different "hick ups" in worship sets; from pages falling off of a music stand due to windy conditions outside, to simply waiting on the rest of the band to get ready to start the next song.

Every church is different regarding their methods of communication in a service. Some churches have the custom of a pastor or ministry leader getting up on the stage with a word of prayer, or a vocal directive for the rest of the congregation. Other churches have portions in the service where announcements are shared in between different songs. You do not want to allow different elements to create Speed Bumps in your service. These communication areas need to be thought of in the context of worship transitions. You should always look to sustain the Inertia of your set. This movement of energy can continue through the music, announcements, the pastor's message and on through the closing of the service.

I highly recommend communicating the song order with your pastor and others who are involved in leading the service. With everyone on the same page, together you can craft a service that directs every person in your congregation to the message God has for your church that day, or just being in His presence. Otherwise, if you look at your service as just getting through the many different segments of announcements / music / offering / prayer, you run the risk of chopping up God's presence into little chunks. We were created to walk with God. That means we need to spend more time with Him. Churchgoers can experience a negative reaction when the Inertia is broken up in a service. Have you ever heard someone say, "this church service feels programmed, devoid of connection, there's no emotion, I didn't feel anything...." We have the potential to hinder the work of the Holy Spirit if we lose sight of how important small transitions are. Keeping that energy flowing can help others connect with God's presence.

It's better to have one clear message when presenting an idea to your church. For example, say you are planning a service about salvation. You develop a set list where each song is focused around God's saving grace. After the music portion, another pastor picks up the ball and connects the announcements with the message of salvation by using a scripture verse relating to the last song you sang. Each announcement is focused on events or service opportunities in the church in helping others find salvation. This leads to a sermon bumper video which sets up your pastor's sermon on salvation. At the close of the message, you play another song in the prayer time inviting others to come forward and receive salvation. Each element in the service is focused on a theme and transitions are rehearsed to seamlessly flow from one to another. You have retained the Inertia and thematic energy.

Smooth transitions help to form cohesive information for your audience, which in turn is much easier to understand and digest. Protecting these moments of moving from one element to another, removing possible distractions, and connecting one element to the next help build a Powerful environment. This is a key factor to bringing people into a state of worship.

I fully believe that God can pour out his Spirit and connect with people within a split second, should He choose. My experience with human nature and several different church cultures however, lead me to believe that it takes a few minutes for most people to let their walls come down. I served as a leader of a multi site church where the length of our worship services was strictly enforced. If the worship band played over the suggested 15 to 18 minutes, one of the pastors walked up in the middle of a song and began speaking on the microphone, welcoming people to the service. I quickly recognized the importance of creating a saturated, concise and smooth worship experience for that amount of time.

No Awkward Silences

No one wants an awkward silence. If you've ever had a first date before then you know what I'm talking about. It's that small amount of time where no one is talking, and you don't know what, or if anything, is going to happen next. It's a strange feeling and most everyone picks up on it. You may have no one looking around. But, you can rest assured everyone is waiting for something to happen or expecting someone to take the lead.

The existence of an awkward silence somehow transcends time and space when you're in show business. A silence that lasts only 3 to 5 seconds, on any normal clock, feels more like an eternity when you're on the stage under the lights. One example of an uncomfortable break like this would be the end of a song, no transition, no action is perceived, and team members are on the stage looking at one another for a cue of what's next. The Worship Leader's goal is to prevent anything like this from happening. We are to lead everyone in the congregation to be supremely focused on God's presence in the room. This way each person may experience God speaking to them individually.

Process to Develop Transitions

There are various methods for creating great musical transitions, and you'll find it's a pretty easy process.

1. Plan out your transitions in your personal practice time.
    a. Without anyone else around, develop the transitions just like the rest of the vision for the service. This is an important part of the plan, so don't leave it out the strategy and development stage.

   b. Practicing / Developing transitions on your own will help you lock-in to your vision without the distraction of thinking about other instruments and elements that will need to be addressed later on.

2. Quickly run from one song to another.
   a. Moving quickly helps you to get a feel for the energy and Inertia you want to keep moving forward.
   b. You may find that you're not in need for much of a transition, especially if the two adjoining songs are in the same key / relative keys and close tempos.

3. Pick out an instrumentalist to lay down some cover to help ease into the next song.
   a. You are looking for some instrumentation that could be available to provide "smoothing over the gap" from one song to another.
   b. Many churches now make a lot of use of pads by "filling in" the sound of most, if not all, worship songs. You can use a variety of synthesizer pads; I generally choose something that is pretty soft and indiscriminate (do not contain an "attack" on the start of the note or chord). There are even apps you can use now that have preprogrammed pad sounds that are ready to go at the push of a button.
   c. Of course, you can use traditional instrumentation like Pianos, ELG with reverb and swell are really nice, or arpeggiating ACG. You can also go wild and have a screaming electric guitar solo, drum solo, or funky bass to lead into the next song. It really depends on what you're coming from and where you are going.
   d. I generally try to match the energy of the previous song to the next, or take that energy and continue to focus it down into a more intimate setting musically.

4. Pick a starting point towards the end of first song that will become the beginning of the transition.
    a. If you're using click tracks, go through this ending without the click track, just play acoustically and model for the rest of the band how you would like the transition to work.
    b. Determine some of the most interesting factors of the end of the song and see if they can continue into the next song. This may be something like a drumbeat, a musical motif, or a musical pad that would just extend from one song to the next.
5. Start the next song with the desired tempo and intensity you want to build into.
    a. Look for a way to blend the ending of the previous song into the beginning of the next song
    b. Direct the musical energy into either continuing along the same path, or focusing into a more intimate musical setting (make the orchestration lighter / take out a couple instruments, soften the volume, bring down the lights a little)

You will want to practice this transition with your team several times. Do not be alarmed if the transition is a trouble spot when first attempted. You will need to go over the challenge and communicate effectively what you want your band members to perform in this section. Rehearse this new area multiple times until you can seamlessly go from one song to the next. Pay close attention to any distractions that may disrupt the flow of energy and readjust your transition accordingly. When you feel the transition is smooth and one element blends into the next without any disruptive characteristics, your work is done and you've created a bridge for the Inertia to continue.

Here are a few more things to keep in mind, other factors to practice with your teams when dealing with transitions:

1. The changing of a Capo on a guitar
2. Changing patches on a Synth / Keyboard
3. Team members switching instruments / different guitars etc.
4. If you're using click tracks - Clicking over to the next song
5. Movement on stage – Pastors / Vocal Soloists / Band Members / Prayer team / or a Children's choir lining up on stage
6. The cue for a video to start
7. The cue for a lighting change

After you have established what your transition is going to be, and you have practiced the transition several times, it's important to play through the ending of the previous song then the transition leading to the Intro / Verse of following song. This may seem like overkill, but I find this gives the team even more confidence in how the transition operates and will be executed in the performance. Practice each transition at least three times and your band will have it down.

Song Ending – Transition – Song Intro to Verse 1 = 3x

Simply repeat these steps for every transition in your set.

The Mark of a Powerful Rehearsal

– Transitions

1. Inertia
2. No Awkward Silences
3. Process to Develop Transitions

CHAPTER 15:
STOP THE CLOCK

A decisive ending to the rehearsal clearly communicates your dedication to the rehearsal plan and Syllabus. Your team will also have greater sense of urgency to stay focused during the time together. Have you ever gone to a meeting or an event where you weren't sure when it was going to end? Time seems to drag on and you lose your enthusiasm for being there. You may start thinking about all the places you would rather be and things you'd rather be doing. I doubt anyone could say they're really being productive when in this state of "meandering thoughts." Without an end in sight to rehearsal, it's incredibly hard to encourage your team to strive to give their best in the present.

Hit the Wall

I enjoy running. Let me rephrase that, I enjoy what running does for me. I push to accomplish exercise goals physically knowing I'll reap benefits both mentally and spiritually. I don't really enjoy the impact on my knees and I can't stand running outside when it's cold. I hate having that feeling in my lungs like ice burning through my insides. However, there have been times where I've gone running on a beautiful day. I've felt the wind in my face, a breeze on my back, and I felt like I could just keep going forever. I didn't want to stop. I imagined myself seeing the world simply by using my own two feet, just like Forrest Gump.

I've often thought about running a marathon. To this date, I haven't done one... yet. I have heard many runners talk about, "The Wall," like it's a real location that every runner encounters. This phenomenon happens to runners around the 18-20-mile mark when their bodies have depleted all their stored-up glycogen (a source of energy). Runners typically experience feelings of fatigue and negativity because they are burning through this carbohydrate stored in their muscles and liver for energy. When your body runs low on this source for energy, even the brain wants to shut down as a preservation method.

Let's check the math here. Our bodies store on average around 1,800 – 2,000 calories worth of glycogen in our muscles and liver. Depending on your body mass and the pace in which you run, you burn about 100 calories per mile. You can see why most people would hit the wall around this same time.

(1,800 to 2,000 calories) ÷ 100 Calories per mile = 18 – 20 miles

I find this next question fascinating. In spite of "Hitting the Wall," how many people finish marathons each year? In 2016, there were 817 marathons scheduled in the United States and Canada. Out of these races, an astounding 505,413 runners completed a full marathon which is 26.2 miles. If a majority of them are facing this common human experience of depleted energy, their bodies actually wanting to shut down, each person experiencing this close to the same time and distance in the race, then how are so many runners finishing the race? What is pushing these runners to complete this goal when their bodies are shutting down, and their thoughts can't help but shout out, "I WANT TO QUIT!"

The only answer I can come up with is, "Our beliefs dictate our actions." Our performance is directly affected by what we believe. My personal best in long distance runs resulted from getting over a barrier in my mind where I thought I couldn't go any longer. I pushed through the hard times when I wanted to give up because I set a goal for myself. When I saw the end, when I knew I only had a little more to go, I actually ran faster and with greater form. I was excited to meet that goal and give my best for that time and distance.

Think about our lives and how Scripture tells us in Hebrews 12:1

"...let us ***run*** *with perseverance* ***the race*** *marked out for us."*

Each one of us are given a certain amount of time here on earth and we are to use our time as God has called us, bringing Him glory. I believe each one of us have an objective and a purpose. Many are aware of the reality that time is short on this side of heaven. If you've ever heard of a person with a near-death experience, their lives sometimes change dramatically afterwards their experience. They often feel an urgency to take action and get something done with the rest of their time in this life. This is a much different picture than someone who has no aspirations, no dreams, no calling, no vision for the future, no pressing needs on them at the present given time. You may imagine this next person sitting around, twiddling their thumbs and waiting for something exciting or out of the ordinary to happen. Remember our definition of Inertia that we discussed earlier?

> ***Inertia*** *- the property of matter by which it retains its state of rest or its velocity along a straight line so long as it is not acted upon by an external force.*

As leaders, God has called us into a great opportunity to do something special for His Kingdom. I am being honest and transparent when I say that *Ministry is a Marathon*. No matter what area of ministry you are in, there will be times when you, "Hit the Wall." You may hit it really hard. Or maybe "The Wall" seemingly attacks you for no reason at all!

I want to encourage you to get back up, keep running. You may have to walk or limp in part of your race. That's OK. Take the time you need to heal and get back on your feet. Find ways to build yourself back up. Find a mentor who can train you and coach you through times of greater challenges. Push yourself to become a greater runner in your individual race. Let "Your Beliefs Dictate Your Actions."

Now back on track with rehearsal practices, ask yourself what are the beliefs of your team? Do they all understand the purpose of being there together? Does your team comprehend what "Worship" is as opposed to just playing music? Do they understand the difference between "practice" and "rehearsal?" Do they believe that You will stop rehearsal On Time, pushing forward to get the most out of the time they've given you? Giving a clear ending to rehearsal will actually fuel passion, energy, focus and concentration during your rehearsal time more than letting it drag on forever. Make sure you communicate a clear ending of the rehearsal. I have found that 6:00 to 8:00 PM often works well for a midweek rehearsal. When I am approaching 8 o'clock, like around 7:50-7:55, I make sure that I am wrapping everything up so that I can end right on the dot. I may even make a few remarks like, "Before we head out of here in a few minutes, I want to go over this section one more time." Or, "Does anyone have any questions before we close for tonight?"

This is a highly important and often forgot about virtue of being a great leader –

"Be Mindful of and Respect Everyone's Time."

I don't know how many meetings, practices and rehearsals I've been to where I was under someone else's leadership and the rehearsal continued on and on. I was to the point where I didn't know if I would ever see home again. I understand wanting to achieve all of the objectives set forth in the leader's syllabus, however I could not help but feel the planning on the front end was poorly managed. Accurate communication had not been given on the time requirements of this rehearsal. I kid you not, I have been to some rehearsals that were advertised as being two hours long and they ended up being well over three hours. By the end of that rehearsal I was getting antsy in my chair, or tired of standing on my feet, and fully frustrated about the lack of proper communication. I felt disrespected by the leader. Their actions communicated to me that my time did not matter, I wasn't important enough to be included or consulted on the time constraints. I remember looking around at the rest of the group, wondering if they were feeling the same as me or if I was just an anomaly that had other things to do. I'm not one to quit and storm off, that's socially frowned upon. But... I've thought about it.

Build Confidence in Your Team

I shared earlier about one of the directives of a leader is instilling confidence in their team. Open and honest communication to your team will speak volumes. Speak to the people on your team! This helps get everyone on the same page. Your team members are there because they made a commitment to you, the church, the rest of the team and they have a desire to see things done well. They want to do well. They want their time to be filled efficiently in rehearsal. They also want to know the leader received the gift of their time as valuable.

Your team members are graciously giving you their weeknight, their weekend, their Sunday morning and any other time when there is a service. They have friends, they have families, they have other people they could be spending this time with and yet here they are working on music with you for a unified purpose. Make sure you receive the gift of their time well. Let them know you appreciate their offering and sacrifice to be at the rehearsal.

Make sure you have given them an efficient amount of substance in the rehearsal. If you have followed all of the steps listed in this book to this point, then you have done your due diligence in rehearsing and driving forward towards a goal of excellence and musical acuity.

Focus on Music

This is not a time to be entirely social. Rehearsal is not a club or a prayer meeting. I don't want to offend anyone by saying that, but if you want to have a prayer meeting then do that at another time when prayer can be the focus, just as rehearsal should be the focus for this time. I am all for having prayer together as a worship team. I believe it is vitally important for a team to be spiritually unified.

You can have prayer at the beginning of rehearsal, at the end, or both. I typically have a short prayer at the beginning of rehearsal, sometimes after the first run through when a few stragglers might still be coming through the door and getting ready. I will have a brief prayer at the end, thanking God for the opportunity to worship Him. I also thank Him for the ability He's given us to use our talents and gifts to lift him up in this rehearsal time. Depending on the individual needs or any big prayer requests known by everyone on the team or the entire church, I'll have everyone come together and gathered for a special time of prayer at the end of the rehearsal. This also helps close out the night on a great spiritual note. Prayer gets everyone on board with what God is going to do through us in the coming service.

Prayer is great. Being social, joking around, building relationships with your team is great. But, stay focused on what your time is primarily for. It's ironic, but you will find your team will naturally gravitate towards more relational aspects as you focus on the music in rehearsal. Your team will find common ground in the aspects of what they are working on together. This will aid in breeding more connections throughout your department.

Be Gracious to your Team

Be Gracious to your Team. We've already gone over this important part a couple of times, but I can't emphasize it enough. Thank them for the time they've given and the effort they put forth in transporting their gear, pedalboards, instruments, driving through the traffic and the snow in the wintertime or adverse weather conditions. Make note of their sacrifice and celebrate it! Make sure to emphasize abundantly how important it is for them to serve and be on the team, and how thankful you are for each one of them.

Applaud them on a job well done. They have given the last two hours to you and have gone through several songs numerous times. Their ability to stay focused, concentrate on the music and enhance their skill set is something to be proud of. You should be able to see your vision for the service coming together. The fact that everyone on the team has given his or her best to fulfill that vision is uplifting. You are not building this Powerful Service on your own. You are growing together as a team. With more practices like this, you will be able to push yourselves farther and become more skilled in the future. The growing never stops.

Recap / Reminder

Remind them of some challenge spots in the music you went over tonight. A little time of reflection, however brief it is, helps to bring forth the important areas of rehearsal in your team's mind. Have you ever asked a small child what they learned in Sunday school or in classes that day? The answers are pretty consistent. I typically hear something like, "I don't remember, I don't know, something..." Not that your team is going to forget everything you've accomplished once they walk out of the building, but a healthy recap of challenges throughout the rehearsal will serve the team well in reminding them what to practice when they go home. Communication is vitally important in everything that we do. I've always heard, "In ministry, you can't Over Communicate!" Recaps / Reminders are especially helpful, used to further instruct your team on what is important, i.e. challenging areas of the music that you want to make sure are done well in the worship service.

I like to give homework to my worship teams. This could be something small, but is a step that will support their progression of skill. Even outside of this rehearsal, you can help each team member achieve victory in those trouble spots before the performance. Below are a few homework ideas you could feel comfortable giving every week to your team. Use these as standards and requirements your worship culture can expect after each rehearsal.

Homework

1. Go home and listen to each song 3X on PCO / iTunes etc. before the service / performance
2. **Look** at your music while **Listening** to the music. Following along in your lead charts / chord charts while listening to the recording of the song will help your mind put the song into greater focus.
   - You'll find that listening to the recording after rehearsal will bring back memories of the rehearsal efforts. You may also develop new ideas of how to achieve a specific sound / rhythm / dynamic contrast
3. Practice Your Part at least 3X before the service / performance

The Mark of a Powerful Rehearsal

- Stop the Clock

1. Hit the Wall
2. Inertia
3. "Be mindful of and Respect Everyone's Time."
4. Build Confidence in Your Team
5. Focus on Music
6. Be Gracious to your Team
7. Recap / Reminder
8. Homework

CHAPTER 16:
CLOSING

Multiple Levels

We've covered a lot of ground regarding sharing your vision and painting a picture of your vision for the team. If you've ever seen the movie Inception, think of your Powerful Rehearsal as, "A painting within a painting, within a painting, within a painting … etc." Your vision for worship has multiple levels. Each level has its own intricate procedures that must be in place, properly understood, and confidently executed to hold up the vision of the next level.

My daughter has this toy she got for Christmas. It's a set of blocks comprised of a box within a box, within a box, etc. There are 5 different boxes altogether. The toy packs up nicely, all concealed within the largest box as each smaller box fits within the one just larger than itself. A wooden shape is included with each individual box which is painted and cut to match a corresponding hole on the side of it's respective box. You have five different pieces in the shape of a square, circle, triangle, rectangle, and star. Every box in the set can neatly fit together in one concise package, or you can use each box to build a tower of that securely fits each box on top of the other in order from

large to small. The top of each box has a small lip around it for a smaller box to fit into. This tower arrangement reveals brightly painted numbers and letters on each side, and don't forget the colorful cutout shape you can place on the inside of each level. This is a multi-faceted toy. Each element has been individually designed, constructed with care, and deliberately proportioned to fit with the other components. You can tell a lot of planning went into how the assembly of each part would together build a bigger toy, and also how each box / level is a compact toy on its own. Without the vision for this toy being carried out under specific measurements, it would not securely stand up. The successive layers wouldn't fit together. If you tried to build the boxes up, it'd probably fall over and crash on the floor.

Another example of Multiple Layers is the body of Christ. The many parts of the body each have their own function and are vital to the health of the body. They are individually significant and also part of one greater form.

Romans 12:4-8 (NIV) 4 For just as each of us has one body
with many members, and these members do not all have the
same function, 5 so in Christ we, though many, form one body,
and each member belongs to all the others. 6 We have different
gifts, according to the grace given to each of us. If your gift is
prophesying, then prophesy in accordance with your faith; 7 if
it is serving, then serve; if it is teaching, then teach; 8 if it is to
encourage, then give encouragement; if it is giving, then give
generously; if it is to lead, do it diligently; if it is to show mercy,
do it cheerfully.

With all of your team members understanding each layered element in the vision, and how they are a support to the larger form, you will have a team united and focused in bringing about the masterpiece God has given to you for this service.

Extra Standard Requirements

Here are just a few extra steps to follow in order to uphold high standards for giving the best every weekend. You can easily remind yourself and your team members of these after each rehearsal. Each of these standards is free. You don't have to pay anything to get them, but they will cost you something. You will have to give up time devoted to yourself, energy focused on needs outside of worship music, and thoughts that are not uplifting to our brothers and sisters in Christ. Following these five standards alone will help you build a thriving culture that is driven to give a Powerful offering of worship.

1. **Be Prepared**
2. **Be On Time**
3. **Be Thorough**
4. **Be Encouraging**
5. **Be Gracious**
6. **Be A Servant**

Your Leadership Development

As you continue to develop your skills as a worship leader every week, month and year, you will find particular things that work really well for you. It's taken me over twenty years to develop the collection of methods and practices included in this book. I am so thankful for the opportunity to share this knowledge with you.

Make sure that you enjoy the journey along the way. You may not hear this encouragement very much in the midst of challenge and conflict, but just remember that God is doing great work through you.

James 1:2 (NIV) - Consider it pure joy, my brothers and sisters, whenever you face trials of many kinds, 3 because you know that the testing of your faith produces perseverance.
4 Let perseverance finish its work so that you may be mature and complete, not lacking anything. 5 If any of you lacks wisdom, you should ask God, who gives generously to all without finding fault, and it will be given to you.

Romans 12:12 (NIV) - Be joyful in hope, patient in affliction, faithful in prayer.

Galatians 6:9 (NIV) - Let us not become weary in doing good, for at the proper time we will reap a harvest if we do not give up.

2 Thessalonians 2:13 (NIV) - And as for you, brothers and sisters, never tire of doing what is good.

Remember that every leader is different. You may find yourself developing systems and plans not listed in this book. That is a great thing! As we each travel our own unique paths, God will bring opportunities for us to change and grow. Your circumstances and challenges may look different than some of the ones I've been through, but don't lose heart. You are not in this alone!

May God bless you to create new practices to overcome your unique challenges. I pray you share your blessing and knowledge with others. I hope that you will go on with everything that you've learned in this book, put it into practice, and Build a Powerful Rehearsal!

The Mark of a Powerful Rehearsal

- Closing

1. Multiple Levels
2. Extra Standard Requirements
3. Your Leadership Development

CHAPTER 17:
RESOURCES

Find These and More Resources Online at Downpourintl.com/Powerhouse

Simple Rehearsal Syllabus

A. Opening / Rehearsal Rundown
B. Song 1
C. Song 2
D. Song 3
E. Song 4
F. Going Back
G. Transitions

Expanded Rehearsal Syllabus

A. **Opening** – Quick Prayer asking God to bless the rehearsal time

1. Start playing the first song at the beginning of rehearsal – Right On Time / when it's supposed to start – 6:00 PM sharp!
2. Welcome Everyone
3. Ask if everyone was able to Practice the songs before rehearsal
4. If someone says No, then you know right away to bring up and address their specific instrument / solo areas in each song.

5. ***Do not leave this up to chance that they'll magically just "get their part!"
6. Discuss the Order of the songs

B. Song 1

1. Make note of the tempo and the "Feel" of the song
2. ELG Solos / Drum Riffs
3. Breakdown section with only drums, vocals continue, everyone claps their hands to get the congregation engaged

C. Song 2

1. Changing who has the solos
2. Possible focus change from ELG to Piano for example
3. Continue to keep the energy up

D. Song 3

1. Focus on areas where Band gives more space for Vocals to come out more

E. Song 4

1. Begin song softly, build in intensity, dies down at the end to same dynamics as beginning

F. Going Back

1. Go back through the set to rework problem areas

G. Transitions

1. Make multiple run-throughs ending one song and beginning next
2. Discuss the Worship Momentum / Inertia of the set with the band

Setting up the Stage Sample Guide

The Stage has Zones

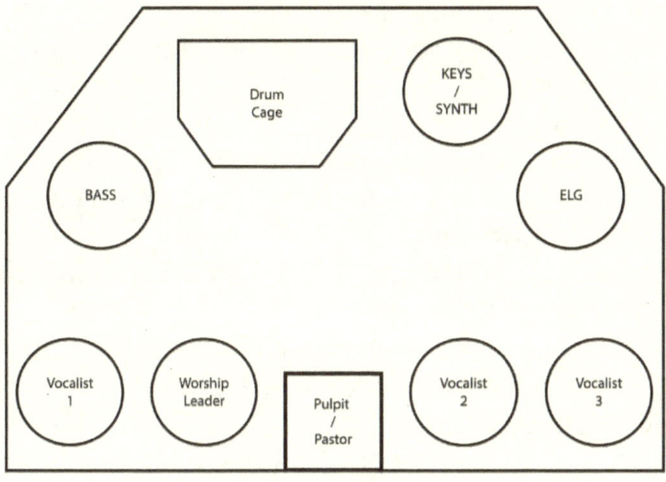

Sound Check Guide

Run Through Stage Zones in Order

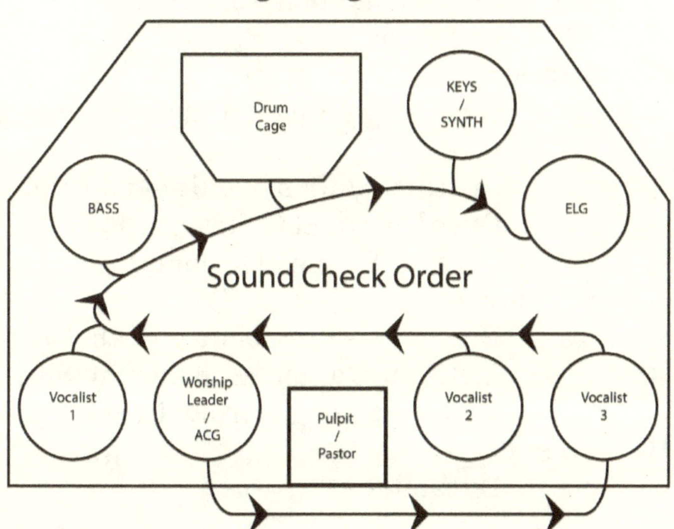

Song Evaluation Guide

A. **Intro**
  a. Dynamics
  b. Instrumentation and Musical Motifs

B. **Verse 1**
  a. Dynamics
  b. Instrumentation
  c. Vocals – Melody / Lead Only Typically

C. **PreChorus**
  a. Dynamics – Soft then Crescendo into Chorus
  b. Instrumentation – Driving Rhythms
  c. Vocals – Add BGV Lightly

D. **Chorus**
  a. Dynamics – 1st time *mf*
  b. Instrumentation – Pull back Instrumentation at start
  c. Vocals – Strong, Add in Harmonies

E. **Intro / Instrumental**
  a. Dynamics – Strong as in the beginning
  b. Instrumentation – Same as in the beginning

F. **Verse 2**
  a. Dynamics – Build up slightly from V1 level
  b. Instrumentation – Add slightly more Overdrive in ELG, Stronger Bass
  c. Vocals – Strong, Harmonies

G. **PreChorus**
  a. Dynamics – Crescendo into Chorus
  b. Instrumentation – Driving Rhythms
  c. Vocals – Strong, Harmonies

H. **Chorus**
  a. Dynamics – *f*

b. Instrumentation – Full Band, Everyone Driving
c. Vocals – Strong, Harmonies

I. **Bridge**
a. Repeats – Multiple, but no more than 3
b. Dynamics - Variations
c. Instrumentation – Highlight a different Instrument / Motif
d. Vocals – Strong, Harmonies

J. **Chorus**
a. Repeats – At Least 2
b. Dynamics - *ff*
c. Instrumentation – Full and Strong
d. Vocals – Strong, Harmonies

K. **Intro / Outro / Instrumental**
a. Dynamics – Same as in Beginning
b. Instrumentation - Same as in Beginning

Process to Develop Transitions

1. Plan out your transitions in your personal practice time.
   a. Without anyone else around, develop the transitions just like the rest of the vision for the service. This is an important part of the plan, so don't leave it out the strategy and development stage.
   b. Practicing / Developing transitions on your own will help you lock-in to your vision without the distraction of thinking about other instruments and elements that will need to be addressed later on.
2. Quickly run from one song to another.
   a. Moving quickly helps you to get a feel for the energy and Inertia you want to keep moving forward.
   b. You may find that you're not in need for much of a transition, especially if the two adjoining songs are in the same key / relative keys and close tempos.
3. Pick out an instrumentalist to lay down some cover to help ease into the next song.
   a. You are looking for some instrumentation that could be available to provide "smoothing over the gap" from one song to another.
   b. Many churches now make a lot of use of pads by "filling in" the sound of most, if not all, worship songs. You can use a variety of synthesizer pads; I generally choose something that is pretty soft and indiscriminate (do not contain an "attack" on the start of the note or chord). There are even apps you can use now that have preprogrammed pad sounds that are ready to go at the push of a button.
   c. Of course, you can use traditional instrumentation like Pianos, ELG with reverb and swell are really

nice, or arpeggiating ACG. You can also go wild and have a screaming electric guitar solo, drum solo, or funky bass to lead into the next song. It really depends on what you're coming from and where you are going.

d. I generally try to match the energy of the previous song to the next, or take that energy and continue to focus it down into a more intimate setting musically.

4. Pick a starting point towards the end of first song that will become the beginning of the transition.
    a. If you're using click tracks, go through this ending without the click track, just play acoustically and model for the rest of the band how you would like the transition to work.
    b. Determine some of the most interesting factors of the end of the song and see if they can continue into the next song. This may be something like a drumbeat, a musical motif, or a musical pad that would just extend from one song to the next.
5. Start the next song with the desired tempo and intensity you want to build into.
    a. Look for a way to blend the ending of the previous song into the beginning of the next song
    b. Direct the musical energy into either continuing along the same path, or focusing into a more intimate musical setting (make the orchestration lighter / take out a couple instruments, soften the volume, bring down the lights a little)

CHAPTER 18:

APPENDIX

The Mark of a Powerful Rehearsal

- Introduction

1. What's the point of a Powerful Rehearsal?
2. Contributing Factors for a Powerful Worship Service include;
   a. Spiritual Unity in the church and use of Familiar and Favorite Worship songs or anthems
   b. New and Exciting aspects for people to look forward to, i.e. - New Songs, God Speaking a New Word and giving Focus to the church leadership
   c. Recognition of how God is moving in this church
   d. Joyful Fellowship and Connections within the church body
   e. Ministry Focused Campaigns for building God's Kingdom and the church as a whole
   f. The Support of all church attendees in the service
   g. A Powerful Rehearsal that prepares all those involved in producing the Worship Service
3. Rehearsal Overview

Chapter 1

– A System for Planning

1. Find a Creative and Effective way to Plan
2. "Creatives" and the Analytical side of the job
3. Online Service Planning
4. Our God is Present in the Moment.
5. Our God is one who plans.

Chapter 2

– One Man Band

1. We are better together.
2. Delegate
3. Who's in Your Band?

Chapter 3

– Click Tracks

1. Produce Your Own
2. Click Track Resources

Chapter 4

– Practice By Yourself

1. Individual Practice
2. Corporate Rehearsal

Chapter 5

– Build Your Syllabus

1. How long should a rehearsal last?
2. What is A Syllabus? – An Outline
3. Simple Rehearsal Syllabus
4. Expanded Rehearsal Syllabus

Chapter 6

– Set The Stage

1. "Get your own gear Right!"
2. Servant Leadership
3. The Stage has Zones
4. Prepare a place for your team

Chapter 7

– Start the Clock

1. Effectively Communicate the Start Time of rehearsal to everyone involved.
2. Make sure you start the rehearsal ON TIME!
3. Enforce the standards after they are set.
4. Make audible notice of people who are Late.
5. Keep track of the time.
6. Be Mindful of Everyone's Time.
7. Prepare a Rehearsal full of Substance
8. Don't Waste Time – Be Purposeful!

Chapter 8

– Talk to Your Team

1. Welcome Your Team
2. The Environment
3. The Leader Sets the Tone
4. Inclusion of All Team Members
5. The Presence of God is Welcoming to All!
6. Connect through Story to Build Community
7. Talk through the Order
8. Talk through the Tough Spots

Chapter 9

– Sound Check

1. The Importance of Sound Check
2. Instruct New Members how to perform a Sound Check
3. Steps to perform a Solid Sound Check

Chapter 10

– Start First Song

1. Talk Through the Song with Your Team
2. Form in Songs
3. Song Rehearsal Process
4. Song Evaluation
5. Talk Through the Song with Your Team
6. 1st Run-Through
7. Status Check
8. Run the Trouble Spot – Communicate
9. Unique Gifts
10. Highlight Specifics
11. Move On

Chapter 11

– Start Next Song

1. Patterns in Musical Technique
2. Confidence

Chapter 12

– Go Through Your Set Backwards

1. Hacking the Mind in Rehearsal
2. Focus on the Challenging Sections
3. Encouragement

Chapter 13

– Take Stock of the Whole Set

1. Creative Flexibility
2. Jesus Our Creator
3. Ask the Right Questions

Chapter 14

– Transitions

1. Inertia
2. No Awkward Silences
3. Process to Develop Transitions

Chapter 15

– Stop the Clock

1. Hit the Wall
2. Inertia
3. "Be mindful of and Respect Everyone's Time."
4. Build Confidence in Your Team
5. Focus on Music
6. Be Gracious to your Team
7. Recap / Reminder
8. Homework

Chapter 16

– Stop the Clock

1. Multiple Levels
2. Extra Standard Requirements
    a. Be Prepared
    b. Be On Time
    c. Be Thorough
    d. Be Encouraging
    e. Be Gracious
    f. Be A Servant
3. Your Leadership Development

Find more resources and training for
Pastors, Worship Pastors,
and Creative Arts Ministries at
Downpourintl.com

www.ingramcontent.com/pod-product-compliance
Lightning Source LLC
LaVergne TN
LVHW051001080826
845145LV00009B/2390